D0216702

Laura Ingalls Wilder

Twayne's United States Authors Series

Kenneth E. Eble, Editor

University of Utah

TUSAS 517

LAURA INGALLS WILDER
(1867–1957)
Photograph courtesy of Laura Ingalls Wilder
Memorial Society, Inc., De Smet, South Dakota.

Laura Ingalls Wilder

By Janet Spaeth

University of North Dakota

Twayne Publishers
A Division of G.K. Hall & Co. • *Boston*

HOUSTON PUBLIC LIBRARY

R0156751706
HUM

Laura Ingalls Wilder

Janet Spaeth

Copyright 1987 by G.K. Hall & Co.
All rights reserved
Published by Twayne Publishers
A Division of G.K. Hall & Co.
70 Lincoln Street
Boston, Massachusetts 02111

Copyediting supervised by Lewis DeSimone
Book production by Janet Zietowski
Book design by Barbara Anderson

Typeset in 11 pt. Garamond
by P&M Typesetting, Inc.,
Waterbury, Connecticut

Printed on permanent/durable acid-free paper
and bound in the United States of America

Library of Congress Cataloging-in-Publication Data

Spaeth, Janet.
  Laura Ingalls Wilder.

  (Twayne's United States authors series ; TUSAS 517)
  Bibliography: p.
  Includes index.
  1. Wilder, Laura Ingalls, 1867–1957—Criticism
and interpretation. I. Title. II. Series.
PS3545.I342Z88   1987   813'.52   87-15
ISBN 0-8057-7501-3

For Kevin, with my love and thanks

Contents

About the Author

Janet Spaeth received her B.A. from the University of New Mexico, her M.L.S. from the University of Oregon, and her Ph.D. from the University of North Dakota. She teaches at the University of North Dakota and has published articles about children's literature in the *Quarterly* of the Children's Literature Association, *Laura Ingalls Wilder Lore, Plainswoman,* and *Great Lakes Review.* She is a member of the Children's Literature Association, the Society of Children's Book Writers, the Popular Culture Association, and the Laura Ingalls Wilder Memorial Society.

Preface

A kind of mystique surrounds Laura Ingalls Wilder. She seemed to have sprung upon the American—and, later, the world—literary scene from the relative obscurity of a Missouri farm with a fully developed talent for writing, and then proceeded to astonish critics by producing volume after volume of books destined to become American classics, the frontier saga of a pioneer childhood.

She appeared to have opened her life to her audience. The main character of her work was a girl named Laura Ingalls, who married another character, Almanzo Wilder. Through the *Little House* books, she told us the story of her odyssey through childhood. The only part of her life her readers were unfamiliar with was the time between the ending of *The First Four Years* and the publication of *Little House in the Big Woods,* but real life is like that—there are stretches of time during which nothing particularly outstanding happens.

But something outstanding was happening. Laura was learning to write. It was a long, hard apprenticeship, served mainly under the tutelage of her daughter, Rose Wilder Lane, who was herself a well-known novelist and journalist. The reason Laura Wilder, farm wife, persevered was that she had something important to say. She had a story to tell.

The differences between the author and her character Laura are not major, nor is the story Wilder told greatly divergent from her own experience. Perhaps she chose not to insist upon the distinction to retain the essential "truth" of the *Little House* story, which is what the pioneer experience was like. Perhaps she felt that forcing labels such as "true" and "made-up" on a theme as large as the one she undertook would only undermine its impact.

So she became, in the public's eye, Laura. If one had to choose an alter ego, it was not a bad choice.

She was Laura, and yet she was not. In writing this book, I have tried to separate the two by referring to the author as *Wilder* and the character as *Laura,* except in the biography chapter, in which *Laura* was the only choice. Almanzo Wilder was not so easy. Wilder called him *Manly,* a name she uses for him only in *The First Four Years.* So he is alternately *Almanzo* and *Manly* as a character; I have referred to him as *Almanzo* when a reference to the person was required. I hope the distinction will be clear in context.

I have also used a system of abbreviations in referring to her books in textual citations. They are:

LHBW	*Little House in the Big Woods* (1953 ed.)
FB	*Farmer Boy* (1953 ed.)
LHP	*Little House on the Prairie* (1953 ed.)
BPC	*On the Banks of Plum Creek* (1953 ed.)
SSL	*By the Shores of Silver Lake* (1953 ed.)
LW	*The Long Winter* (1953 ed.)
LTP	*Little Town on the Prairie* (1953 ed.)
THGY	*These Happy Golden Years* (1953 ed.)
FFY	*The First Four Years* (1971 ed.)

I have chosen to deal with her works thematically, rather than working with them individually, in deference to Wilder's wishes that the *Little House* books be considered as a multivolume historical novel, although *Farmer Boy,* because it is the only book in which Laura does not appear, is dealt with in a separate chapter.

The significance of Laura Ingalls Wilder's work extends beyond the literary. She has preserved within the pages of the *Little House* books a part of our American heritage—the pioneer experience.

Janet Spaeth

University of North Dakota

Acknowledgments

Material from the Rose Wilder Lane papers at the Herbert Hoover Presidential Library, West Branch, Iowa, used with permission of Roger Lea MacBride.

Photograph of Laura Ingalls Wilder used with permission of Laura Ingalls Wilder Memorial Society, Inc., De Smet, South Dakota.

Portions of Chapter 5 originally appeared in "Language of Vision and Growth," by Janet Spaeth, *Great Lakes Review* 8, no. 1 (Spring 1982):20–24.

I would also like to extend my personal appreciation to the following for their help and enthusiastic encouragement: Vivian Glover of the Laura Ingalls Wilder Memorial Society, Inc., De Smet, South Dakota; Dwight M. Miller of the Herbert Hoover Presidential Library; and William T. Anderson. In addition, I would like to thank the greatly supportive and patient people at Twayne Publishers, and my field editor, Prof. Kenneth E. Eble, who guided this book with his perceptive comments. And last but not least, I would like to express my gratitude to the staff of the Interlibrary Loan Department of the Chester Fritz Library, University of North Dakota, who accomplished miracles without which this book would not have been possible.

Chronology

1938 *On the Banks of Plum Creek* named Newbery Honor Book.

1939 *By the Shores of Silver Lake.*

1940 *The Long Winter. By the Shores of Silver Lake* named Newbery Honor Book.

1941 *Little Town on the Prairie. The Long Winter* named Newbery Honor Book.

1942 *By the Shores of Silver Lake* awarded Pacific Northwest Library Young Reader's Choice Award. *Little Town on the Prairie* named Newbery Honor Book.

1943 *These Happy Golden Years.*

1944 *These Happy Golden Years* named Newbery Honor Book.

1949 Almanzo Wilder dies.

1953 *Little House* books reissued with new illustrations by Garth Williams.

1954 Laura Ingalls Wilder Award established; Laura Ingalls Wilder presented with first award.

1957 Laura Ingalls Wilder dies on 10 February.

1962 *On the Way Home.*

1971 *The First Four Years. Little House* books issued in paperback.

1974 *West from Home.*

Chapter One
Laura's Own Story

The name of Laura Ingalls Wilder has become part of the great saga of the American frontier. Her *Little House* books are based upon her own life (with the exception of *Farmer Boy,* which is based upon her husband's boyhood), and are thus true—to an extent. Whenever a novelist employs a protoganist who is quite like herself, the two frequently become confused in the mind of the reading public. This is especially the case with the *Little House* books, for the main character bears the name of the author. The difficulty is compounded by Wilder's statement that the stories in the books are true.[1] Truth is a term with many meanings, but it must be recognized that literal truth—"facts"—was not what Wilder meant. She was, instead, referring to a metaphorical truth, the capturing of the fundamental essence of experience.[2]

The confusion of protagonist and author resulted in a mass of supposedly biographical articles about Wilder, particularly during the years that the television show "Little House on the Prairie" was a nationwide success. Many of these articles simply retold the sequence of events from the books, presuming that all of it was factual.

Much of it was. But Wilder's intention in writing the *Little House* series—"I wanted the children now to understand more about the beginning of things, to know what is behind the things they see—what it is that made America as they know it"[3]—demanded a refashioning of the events of her life to retain the larger truth that she wanted to convey—the pioneer experience in America. That some of it is fiction, or adapted fact, in no way detracts from the success of her work. Nor does it make the story of the "Little Houses" any less "truthful." If anything, it makes the story more representative of the overall experience of pioneering.

Laura Ingalls Wilder's own story should start with her parents.[4] Charles Philip Ingalls was born in New York in 1836. His family moved to Illinois when he was twelve years old, and then to Wisconsin when he was nineteen.

It was there that he met Caroline Lake Quiner. Her parents had come from Connecticut to Wisconsin, where she was born in 1839. Her father died when she was still a little girl, and her mother struggled to keep the family together. They moved to another location in Wisconsin two years after Caroline's father died, and there her mother met and married Frederick Holbrook.

After teaching school for a few years, Caroline married Charles Ingalls on 1 February 1860. About two years later, they moved, along with his family, to the Big Woods area of Wisconsin near Pepin, where they all shared a large house.

In 1863, Charles bought land of his own and built a small house on it. In 1865, Charles and Caroline's first daughter, Mary Amelia, was born, and on 7 February 1867, Laura Elizabeth Ingalls was born.

There were already Ingallses in the area when Charles and Caroline moved to the Big Woods with his family, so they did not lead an isolated existence—on the contrary, there were large parties and plenty of help was available. Soon, Charles began to feel that there were too many people, and he decided that it was time to move on.

Charles and his brother Henry had purchased land in Missouri, and in 1868, the two families went south. They stayed for a year, and then Henry and his family returned to the Big Woods of Wisconsin. Charles and his family moved westward, on to Kansas, to Indian Territory.

The land there was all that Charles had dreamed of, but it could not belong to him: the Osage Indians had title to it. In 1870, the United States Army began removing settlers from the area, many of whom, like Charles, had been led to believe the land was available.

The Osage tribe signed a new treaty with the United States government, but the Ingalls family did not stay. The man who had bought their cabin and land in Wisconsin wrote them, asking them to take it back, so the Ingalls family returned to the Big Woods of Wisconsin. This time there were five of them, for another daughter, Caroline Celestia, had been born in Kansas in 1870.

The Big Woods had changed. It was becoming heavily populated with settlers, and in the crowded woods, hunting was poor. It was soon time for the Ingalls family to go West.

In 1874, Laura and her family settled in Walnut Grove, Minnesota, on the edge of Plum Creek. Their first home was a dugout, a house carved out of a hillside. The town of Walnut Grove was just beginning that year, and it was growing rapidly. Soon there was a church, and then a school. One of Laura's schoolmates was Nellie Owens, whose father owned the store in Walnut Grove.

Plum Creek and Walnut Grove seemed like the place where the Ingalls family could settle at last—not only were there a church and a school; the town was served by a railroad. The crops looked promising, and it appeared that prosperity had come to the Ingalls family. But two years of grasshopper plagues destroyed the crops and consumed most of the natural vegetation in the area. Even the water was tainted by the bodies of the insects. The grasshoppers had ravaged not only the land, but the dreams of the settlers.

The Ingalls family's resources were depleted, and they had another mouth to feed. On 1 November 1875, a son, Charles Frederick, was born.

The family decided to move again, this time to Burr Oak, Iowa, where Charles and Caroline had agreed to run the Masters Hotel. The Ingallses stopped along the way to visit Laura's Uncle Peter and Aunt Eliza, who lived near South Troy, Minnesota. It was while they were there that Laura's little brother died.

The Ingalls family spent nearly two years in Burr Oak. Laura later remembered it as "a lovely place," recalling in particular the bullet hole in the door of the hotel, her school days there, and walks in the pasture and the cemetery with a friend.[5] While they were in Burr Oak, another daughter, Grace Pearl, was born in 1877.

Despite Laura's fond remembrances, her parents were not happy in Burr Oak. Charles was working, but he could not seem to earn enough to support them. It was time to move again. They decided to return to Walnut Grove. There the family faced another disaster. Mary became severely ill and, after suffering a stroke, lost her sight.

The family was undoubtedly worn out from the trials of the past few years. It seemed as if tribulation in the form of sickness and debt haunted their footsteps, no matter where they went. Just when life looked bleakest, Charles's sister Docia arrived—with a solution.

Her husband, Hiram, worked for the railroad, and he needed someone to help him take care of the store and the books and the payroll. The pay was steady, and best of all, it was west—in the Dakota Territory. It meant another move, but Charles promised Caroline that this would be the last.

After some time at the railroad's Silver Lake camp, about forty miles west of Brookings in what is now South Dakota, Charles filed a homesteading claim. Instead of moving to the claim immediately, the family took up quarters in the surveyors' house, in exchange for Charles's looking after the railroad's property during the winter.

The next spring, a stream of people came to the area, and the surveyors' house became an improvised hotel. A town, De Smet, was quickly growing up near them, and people needed places to stay. Anticipating the needs of a growing community, Charles began to build a store in town, and in April the family left the surveyors' house and moved into town.

They did not stay there long, because they heard stories of claim jumpers and of a man who had died just outside of town, shot by a claim jumper. Quickly Charles built a shanty, and the family moved to their claim.

There was much work to be done—the ground had to be broken, hay mowed from the Big Slough, cottonwoods planted, and the house on the claim and the store in town finished. Laura helped her father as much as she could, for if he failed, they all failed.

An early blizzard proved how little protection a claim shanty offered, and the family moved to the store in town, to be closer to other people and whatever foodstores they might need for the winter. It was a wise move, for the winter of 1880–81 is still remembered as one of the worst on record. Blizzards howled through the small new town, seeming to taunt the residents with an occasional respite, only to reattack with renewed vigor and force. The Ingalls family was fortunate to be in town near other people, but the food supply there was running dangerously low, because the blizzards prevented the trains from bringing in fresh provisions. People were reduced to eating their seed wheat, a precious commodity that held their hopes for the future. Fuel ran low, and the Ingalls family often spent their time twisting hay into small bundles to burn. The hay burned so quickly that making the hay twists was nearly a fulltime job.

A young man whom Laura had met earlier would not let the townspeople starve. Almanzo Wilder undertook a perilous ride through the treacherous weather to get wheat for the numbed community. He and his brother Royal also risked their lives hauling hay. Laura later noted, during the writing of *The Long Winter,* that "only a few . . . kept normal and very much alive. Pa and the Wilder boys did. The others cowered in the houses."[6]

When the hard winter finally drew to an end, the Ingalls family returned to their claim. Almanzo was a frequent visitor to the Ingalls home, and Laura often rode in his buggy behind the matched set of Morgans.

When Laura was fifteen, she received her teaching certificate, although she was under the age required by law. Within two weeks she was teaching at the Bouchie school, the first of the three teaching positions she held while in De Smet. It was too far for her to live at home, so she boarded with the Bouchie family. Almanzo surprised her by driving her home and back each weekend. It was on one of these rides that they gave each other the nicknames they used the rest of their lives: Manly and Bess (from Laura's middle name, Elizabeth, for Almanzo had a sister named Laura).

By this time Almanzo was definitely courting Laura. They spent many enjoyable weekend hours riding across the prairie in Almanzo's buggy, and one evening Almanzo asked her, "Do you want an engagement ring?" She answered,

"That would depend on who gave it to me."
"If I should give it to you?"
"Then it would depend on the ring."[7]

The ring must have met with her approval, for on 25 August 1885, they were married.

Almanzo had filed a homestead claim and a tree claim, and he built a small house that Laura loved. Their first years together were a combination of great happiness and great trouble. The happiness was Rose, their daughter, born 9 December 1886.

The troubles were many. In addition to a bout with diphtheria that left Almanzo permanently lame, the death of a newborn son in 1889, the loss of the homestead claim, and a fire that destroyed their house on the tree claim, a drought had begun. Crop after crop failed, and the trees on the claim died, forcing Almanzo into deep debt and preemption.

Finally they left De Smet in 1890 and stayed a year in Spring Valley, Minnesota, with Almanzo's parents. From there they moved to Westville, Florida, but in 1892 they returned to De Smet.

Laura's parents and Mary had left the claim and moved to town, and Laura and Almanzo and Rose lived near them. Laura sewed to make enough money for the three of them to leave De Smet. Dakota's charm was spent, and they were lured by the promise of Missouri, "The Land of the Big Red Apple."

They left De Smet in 1894, and as they traveled to Missouri, Laura kept notes of the trip in a diary penned in a little notepad. Although she mourned her lack of "an artist's hand or a poet's brain" to record the beauty of a site on the James River, her impression of the area foreshadowed her later skill at description; the bluffs, she wrote, were "gigantic brown waves tumbled and tossed about."[8] Later she described some Nebraska trees: "The sand had drifted away from them until the tree trunks stood up higher than my head, tiptoe on their bare, gnarled roots."[9] When they arrived in Missouri, she characterized the land as "a drowsy country that makes you feel wide awake and alive but somehow contented."[10]

Almanzo and Laura settled in southern Missouri, near Mansfield, on a plot of land that they felt was perfect for them. At first they lived in a small cabin on the site, but soon they built a house, Rocky Ridge Farm, which included many of Almanzo's innovations.

The prior owner had purchased several apple trees and left them, and, in the spirit of "The Land of the Big Red Apple," Almanzo devoted himself to his orchards. Laura concentrated on chickens, priding herself on her hens' ability to produce eggs.

Curiously, the chickens were, in a roundabout way, responsible for her writing career. Because she was so successful in her poultry endeavors, she was frequently requested as a speaker at farm organization meetings. On one occasion she was unable to attend and present her speech, so she sent it to be read by someone else.

Among those who heard her speech read that day was John Case, editor of the *Missouri Ruralist,* a magazine about farming and rural life. He was impressed by what he had heard and contacted her about writing for the magazine.[11] On 18 February 1911, her article "Favors the Small Farm Home" appeared in the magazine. Two articles, "The Story of Rocky Ridge Farm" and "My Apple Orchard," later appeared there under the by-line "A. J. Wilder." It is doubtful that Almanzo wrote these himself; they were probably a collaborative effort between him and Laura.

By the summer of 1912, Laura's name had begun to appear on the masthead of the *Missouri Ruralist* as the editor of the home section, and she soon had her own column. It was an association that lasted twelve years.

Laura and her daughter were developing parallel careers. Besides writing for magazines, Rose was on the staff of a San Francisco newspaper, the *Bulletin,* and Laura, in addition to her work at the *Missouri*

Ruralist, had found markets in the *State Farmer* and two Saint Louis publications, the *Star* and the *Globe Democrat.* When the World's Fair opened in San Francisco in 1915, Rose urged her mother to visit her and her husband, Gillette Lane. As she told her mother in a letter written early that year, not only would they "play together"; Rose would introduce her to new writing vistas. [12]

The first work mother and daughter did together was for the *Bulletin,* writing for the newspaper's "Tuck'em In Corner," a children's poetry column. Although the poems often appeared under the by-line of "The Hush-a-Bye Lady," Rose and Laura's names were also frequently used.

With her daughter's encouragement and help, Laura began publishing in other journals. In June 1919, she espoused the role of the farm wife as an equal partner in an article, "The Farmer's Wife Says," part of the "Whom Will You Marry?" series in *McCall's Magazine.* This fueled Rose's staunch belief that her mother should expand her writing horizons, and thus began a lengthy relationship between the two as editor and writer, teacher and student—and, frequently, cajoler and immovable object.

After the 17 January 1925 issue of the *Country Gentleman* carried Laura's article "My Ozark Kitchen," Rose dismissed Laura's recurring concern that Rose's extensive editing had cast a shadow of doubt over which of them had really done the writing. An exasperated Rose wrote her that the work she had done on Laura's article was "an ordinary re-write job," and that her mother, "like a frolicsome dog that won't stand still to listen," was going to have to pay attention to her advice, for she had learned about writing for the larger markets through experience, experience she was willing to share. Rose ended the lecture with a typical daughter's complaint: "Just because I was once three years old you honestly oughtn't to think I'm never going to know anything." [13]

"The Farm Kitchen" was followed by "The Farm Dining Room," after which there was a lull in Laura's publishing. She was, however, keeping busy. Not only was she an active clubwoman; she had been working as the secretary-treasurer of the Mansfield Farm Loan Association, handling low-interest loans to local farmers, a job she held until 1927.

Another project soon captured her attention: writing the story of her life. She had been considering it for some time, and when Rose came to Rocky Ridge Farm for an extended stay, the two began to work on it in earnest. Laura penciled the drafts on inexpensive "Fifty-Fifty" lined school tablets, thriftily writing on both sides of the paper. "Pioneer Girl," which told of her childhood on the frontier, was finished in 1930.

Among Rose's friends whom Laura had met in San Francisco was a "little artist girl," Berta Hoerner Hader.[14] She and her husband Elmer had since established themselves in the children's picture book field as writers and illustrators. The Haders and Rose and Laura discussed the possibility of turning the "Tuck'em In Corner" poems into a book, and developed the idea of shortening "Pioneer Girl" and trying to publish it as a picture book.

"When Grandma Was a Little Girl" was the title of the abridged version. When Berta Hader showed her copy of the manuscript to a friend of hers, Marion Fiery, who was the editor of the children's department at the publishing house of Alfred A. Knopf, she set in motion the chain of events that led to the publication of the first of the *Little House* books.

Fiery liked the manuscript and asked Laura if she could expand it. Rose offered "Pioneer Girl," but Fiery rejected it. Fiery wanted the story contained in "When Grandma Was a Little Girl," and proposed changes that contributed to the appeal of the later series, such as the inclusion of greater detail and a change in the title.

Most of the transactions concerning "Little House in the Woods," as it was then titled, were handled by Rose and her agent George Bye. On 17 September 1931, a formal offer of acceptance was rendered by Fiery, but complications arose. The children's department at Knopf was being dismantled, and Fiery recommended that they search for another publisher.

The manuscript ended up in the hands of Virginia Kirkus, editor of the children's department at Harper and Brothers. On 26 November 1931, a telegram arrived at Rocky Ridge Farm notifying Laura that Harpers had accepted the book. It was Thanksgiving Day.

The book was rushed into production by the editors at Harpers, who hoped that this would be the "miracle book that no depression could stop."[15] Illustrated by Helen Sewell, a popular children's book artist, *Little House in the Big Woods,* as it had been retitled, seemed to be that "miracle book." Even before it was published on 6 April 1932, it was chosen as a Junior Literary Guild selection.

It was an immediate success, and the *Little House* series began.

Readers awaited anxiously for the saga to continue, and Laura obliged them: first with *Farmer Boy*, the story of Almanzo's childhood on a New York farm, in 1933; then *Little House on the Prairie* in 1935, *On the Banks of Plum Creek* in 1937, *By the Shores of Silver Lake* in 1939, *The Long Winter* in 1940, *Little Town on the Prairie* in 1941, and *These Happy Golden Years* in 1943. As always, Rose worked with her mother, providing editing and advice.

The books were so popular that honors were heaped upon them and Laura. Five of her books were Newbery Honor Books: *On the Banks of Plum Creek, By the Shores of Silver Lake, The Long Winter, Little Town on the Prairie,* and *These Happy Golden Years. By the Shores of Silver Lake* was also presented the Pacific Northwest Library Young Reader's Choice Award in 1942. In 1954, a special honor was accorded Laura. The Association for Library Services established an award recognizing the achievement of an author or illustrator who had made, through his or her lifetime's work, a lasting contribution to children's literature. Laura was the first recipient of the award, which was named in her honor: the Laura Ingalls Wilder Award.

Libraries were named after her. The Detroit Public Library created the Laura Ingalls Wilder Branch Library, and in Pomona, California, the children's section of the public library was called the Laura Ingalls Wilder Room. Even her hometown of Mansfield recognized her by naming its library for her.

In the midst of these accolades and the onrush of public affection, which flooded her mailbox with letters from as far away as Japan, her joy was marred by the death of Almanzo in 1949.

Laura's health began to fail, and on 10 February 1957 she died. She is buried beside her husband and daughter in the cemetery in Mansfield, Missouri.

Interest in her story did not die with her, however. In 1962, her diary of the trip from De Smet to Mansfield was edited and published as *On the Way Home.* Then, after the death of her daughter in 1968, another manuscript was discovered. *The First Four Years,* the story of the struggle Laura and Almanzo faced during the early period of their marriage, was published in 1971. In 1974, *West from Home,* a collection of letters from Laura and Rose to Almanzo during Laura's 1915 visit to San Francisco, appeared.

A long-running television program, "Little House on the Prairie" and its successor, "Little House on the Prairie: A New Beginning" (which together ran from 1974 to 1983 on NBC), caused great distress among dedicated *Little House* fans, because of the liberties the programs took with the books. They were, however, responsible for fostering many people's interest in the saga of a pioneer childhood on the frontier of America in the late 1800s—and for Laura, that would be another honor.

Chapter Two
Family Folklore in
Little House in the Big Woods

One of the outstanding features of the *Little House* series is the sense of family that runs throughout. It is first established in *Little House in the Big Woods,* the book that opens the series. Folklore is a means of identifying a close group, and the folkloric elements in *Little House in the Big Woods* help to characterize the particularly tightly knit Ingalls family. Folklore is also a unifying agent, for it emphasizes the thread of relationship that ties a group—in this case, the Ingalls family—together. Although folklore is sometimes considered the product of comparatively large organizational structures such as tribes or other societies, Alan Dundes, an eminent folklorist, considers the family to be the smallest unit of folkloric activity.[1] In attempting to define "folklore," Francis Lee Utley calls attention to Marius Barbeau's definition, which stresses the "domain" of folklore as the family and community.[2]

Folkloric traditions within a family may range from basic folk beliefs, such as curatives or remedies, to family customs, such as nicknames, game playing, or joking, to more structured and intricate systems, such as the telling of stories or tales. In families, as in other homogeneous groupings, storytelling often develops into a disciplined, almost regulated form of folklore. Certain customs governing storytelling are created within the family, and, although they may be unspoken rules, they are followed rigorously. Storytelling becomes a ritual. It is interesting to note that even in varying cultures, storytelling customs are often the same, dependent upon and regulated by climate, season, family roles, and even the time of day.

As a little girl, Laura Ingalls Wilder listened to her father tell stories, stories that were "too good to be altogether lost."[3] These tales became the structure of *Little House in the Big Woods,* and with the inclusion of other family traditions, establish the atmosphere of "family" and supply a vivid image of the sociological functioning of family members in a frontier household.

Taken by themselves, Pa's stories are not particularly unusual or spellbinding. But by placing the tales in the environment of a child and showing how that child, Laura, reacts to them, Wilder added a dimension to the otherwise rather ordinary stories. This re-creation of the atmosphere of the storytelling surroundings is important to the vitality of the tale. As folklorist Bronislav Malinowski observes, "The text, of course, is extremely important, but without the context it [the tale] remains lifeless. . . . The interest of the story is vastly enhanced and it is given its proper character by the manner in which it is told."[4]

The events of *Little House in the Big Woods* span a year, beginning and ending in autumn. This was a conscious decision. When the manuscript was first seriously considered by Marion Fiery, the children's book editor at Knopf, it was in the form of a book for younger readers entitled "When Grandma Was a Little Girl." Fiery suggested that it be expanded into a book for older readers,[5] and Rose Wilder Lane, who was assisting her mother with the book, recommended that the book's scope be increased from one winter to one year.[6]

Consistent with traditional storytelling patterns in American and European communities, Pa tells stories only in winter and only at night (*LHBW*, 116). The custom of storytelling as a wintertime activity is, as one might suspect, commonly found in northern climates, where winter means shorter days and longer nights, and the cold and the early dark prohibit outdoor play. Storytelling fills the gap between dusk and bedtime, acting as a possible deterrent to the very real danger of "cabin fever." Since the four tales Pa tells, which are set off formally from the text by individual titles, are winter-told stories, they appear only in the first half of the book. Although they are unique tales to the Ingalls family, they repeat themes and motifs common to all societies.

The Ingalls family, like other self-sufficient groupings, follows a daily regimen of ordered work and play. Storytelling is a nighttime activity, occurring after the chores are done and the dinner eaten, and only Pa is recognized as storyteller,[7] a traditional position of leadership. Pa's use of family members in the tales is effective because it brings the stories into a sharper focus for the Ingalls children. This inclusion of people that the children know, particularly when those people are relatives, places Pa's stories in the realm of family oral history, thus tightening the sense of family and tradition that marks the books.

The first of Pa's stories, "The Story of Grandpa and the Panther," which introduces the storytelling tradition in the Ingalls home, is a form of the cautionary tale, warning Laura and Mary about the perils of the woods. The inspiration for the story is Black Susan, the cat who is curled up by the fireplace, serenely gazing into the flames. Black Susan symbolizes the mood of peacefulness in the home. But the cat in Pa's story, however genetically related to Black Susan, is not an emblem of familial orderliness: the panther is a symbol of the wildness of the outdoors. Pa takes an "inner" symbol and makes it an "outer" symbol, creating an opposition of inner/outer, safe/dangerous, home/wilderness, a dichotomous ordering that appears as a major theme consistently throughout the book. Black Susan is positive and mild: the panther is negative and violent.

The culmination of the tale, in which Grandpa barely escapes a panther by running into the safety of his own house, is one that emphasizes the "order out of chaos" view of the wilderness dweller, the culture creator, for without the sanctuary Grandpa's home offered, Laura's grandfather would have been killed by the panther. The inner/outer dichotomy is expanded to include the concepts of controlled/uncontrolled through the introduction of the gun. The outer world, the woods, is filled with violence and potential harm and must be restrained if the inner world, the home, is to be maintained. In Pa's view the gun is the implement necessary for human beings, who are inhabitants of the inner world, to exist in the outer world, for it increases their chances for survival and allows them some degree of control over the dangers of the outer world.

The role of human being as tamer (i.e., controller) is illustrated by Black Susan's "stretching herself before the fire and running her claws out and in" (*LHBW*, 39), for a house cat is a tamed cousin of the panther. The difference between the two cats is marked by their uses of their claws: for Black Susan, extension of the claws signifies satisfaction and contentment; for the panther, it signifies danger and predation.

The second of the stories, "The Story of Pa and the Voice in the Woods," further illuminates the storytelling ritual in the Ingalls home. It is prefaced by an informational passage about making bullets, which Pa does preceding each evening's stories (*LHBW*, 45). The bullet-making passage not only introduces the topic of the story, but at the same time, provides a link with the preceding tale when Pa refers to the necessity of killing a panther with one shot, for a wounded animal is capable of turning on its human hunter and killing him or her before the gun can be reloaded (*LHBW*, 52).

"The Story of Pa and the Voice in the Woods" is a teaching tale. When he was a child, Pa was supposed to bring the cows back from the woods each afternoon. His father had told him not to dawdle along the way; he must be careful to return before nightfall, for there were dangerous animals in the woods. His ignoring of that advice led to the central problem of the tale in which Pa, as a child, was scared by a voice in the nighttime woods. The story acts as a way of teaching Laura and Mary that they must listen to their parents, particularly their father, for parents know from experience what is dangerous.

Audience reaction is an important aspect of storytelling,[8] and at one point in the story, Wilder interrupts Pa's narrative to supply Laura's role in the family's storytelling tradition, which is to prompt him when he pauses in the story (*LHBW*, 57–58). Her anticipation of the story line indicates that this tale is a familiar one to Laura and that she regularly plays an active role in the telling; the pause occurs at the same point in the story each time Pa tells it.

The "punch line" of the story reiterates the educational aspect of the story, emphasizing parental wisdom and knowledge. Pa's father points out to him that the entire incident would not have happened if Pa had obeyed him. The story has a "moral": children should heed the rules established by their parents.

The third story, "The Story of Grandpa's Sled and the Pig," is an explanatory tale and results from Laura's tantrum on a day when she is forced by custom to remain inactive: "I hate Sunday!" (*LHBW*, 86) she shouts in an irreverent outburst. Pa tells her a story about the time her grandfather broke the rule of Sunday rest and got into trouble with his father. The tale is overtly an educational one, designed to show Laura that her present strictures are not nearly so bad as those her grandfather had to accept, and that, in fact, she would have found Sundays more confining had she been a little girl during her grandfather's childhood (*LHBW*, 96).

The second and third stories undoubtedly share a special appeal for the young Laura: in both, the character who misbehaves is not only someone she knows and who is a relative, but someone she respects. The two tales illustrate that these two adults were once children like herself who occasionally disobeyed their parents. Laura enjoys hearing about their escapades, not only because they are exciting, but because such stories probably make her feel better about herself as a child, while she also derives a certain quite human satisfaction from hearing about the mistakes of others. In addition, these tales show Pa's instinctive recognition that children need reassurance that making errors in judgment is a very normal part of childhood.

The last of the tales Pa tells is introduced with more complexity than the others, and reflects deep social patterning. "The Story of Pa and the Bear in the Way" is told the day after Ma and Laura's exciting nighttime adventure, which occurred while Pa was in town. When Ma and Laura went to milk Sukey, the cow, Ma saw a dark shape at the barnyard gate, and thinking it was Sukey, slapped her to make her move. The light from the lantern Laura held then revealed that Ma had slapped not Sukey, but a bear.

The following evening, Pa tells Laura and Mary that he has a "new story" to tell them, "The Story of Pa and the Bear in the Way." The night before, when he was walking home from town, he saw a bear in the woods. It would not move, no matter how he shouted and waved at it. He had to pass it, so he took up a big stick, charged it, and clubbed it on the head. It still did not move: he had clubbed not a bear, but an old burned tree stump.

His story, the events of which occur at the same time as Ma's adventure, and with the same "participant," a bear, is the reverse of hers. Pa's story draws excitement from Ma's adventure, perhaps to divert the children's attention from the real bear, diminishing any fears that they might have about the safety of their home. When Laura asks Pa if he would have clubbed it on the head, had it been a real bear, he answers, "Yes, I would. You see, I had to" (*LHBW*, 115). Not only have Pa's territorial homestead rights been abridged by the infringement of the wild upon his home, but his image as guardian of the home has been challenged. He must reassert his place as the family's protector.

Storytelling does not end in *Little House in the Big Woods* with the last titled tale, but formal storytelling is over with the end of winter. The story of Charley and the bees is told in late summer, during harvest, and is told in the wagon, soon after the events have occurred. It operates outside the traditions of the formal storytelling ritual because it is a tale that gains value by its immediacy.

The story is introduced in the preceding chapter with Pa's bringing home honey. When Laura asks him if any of the bees stung him, he

tells her that they never do (*LHBW,* 197). They do, of course, sting
young Charley, Laura's ten-year-old cousin, and quite badly, but
Charley is not an adult male responsible for a home and a family. In
Laura's eyes, Pa is immune because he is a father.

The story of Charley and the bees is a reworking of "the boy who
cried wolf" tale, except that Charley is confronted by bees instead of
a wolf. But this aspect of it escapes Laura: she sees only Charley's
naughtiness in disobeying his father and slowing down the men's
work.

Charley, who was supposed to be helping the men with the harvest, repeatedly stood at the far end of the field and jumped up and
down and shouted to attract the workers' attention. Each time, the
men dropped their work and ran to him, fearing that he had been
hurt. But Charley only laughed at them for falling for his joke. The
men, finally disgusted with Charley's antics, ignored him the fourth
time he called, but when his cries persisted, they realized something
was wrong: Charley had been jumping on a yellow jackets' nest.

Pa says of the incident, "It served the little liar right" (*LHBW,*
211), but when Laura lies awake that night, she wonders why Pa said
that. She cannot understand why Pa has chosen to focus on Charley's
being a liar, "when he had not said a word" (*LHBW,* 211). Any relationship between Charley and the bees and another boy and a wolf
has passed unnoticed by Laura.

The fact that the main character of this story, Charley, is her
cousin and that Laura knows both him and the setting (only a short
distance separates the two during the incident, for Laura is in the
yard and Charley in the fields) is probably responsible for her misin-
terpreting the story. The use of recognizable figures or a known setting in a story can result in the listener's placing a greater emphasis
on the incident of the story than on the import.[9] The latter is often
clearer when the story is set in the stylized backdrop of the folktale
than in the sharply defined present. Pa's other stories also use characters Laura knows, but she must imbue the stories with her own imagination, for she is not familiar with either her father or her
grandfather as young boys, nor has she been in the woods at night.
The visualization of the characters or the setting must be produced
by her own imagination.

One tale, which the children are not supposed to hear, is that told
by Uncle Peter and Aunt Eliza (*LHBW,* 67–72) after Laura and Mary
and their cousins have gone to bed. Uncle Peter and Aunt Eliza's tale

is not unlike Pa's stories: it is the recounting of a near escape from a dangerous animal. But in the style of the best storytellers, Uncle Peter and Aunt Eliza do not reveal the nature of the danger until the end; rather, they draw the audience's attention to Prince, the family dog, as if he were the dangerous animal, and it is this purposeful misfocusing that captures Laura's initial interest, because Laura "always liked to hear about dogs" (*LHBW,* 67).

For three and a half pages, Uncle Peter and Aunt Eliza tell about Prince's acting mad: he tore at Aunt Eliza's dress and would not let her out of the house. All the detail of the story is focused on Prince's seemingly rabid behavior, and not until the denouement is the reason for his action given: a panther has been lurking outside the house. Uncle Peter and Aunt Eliza, like Pa, are concerned with the threat the uncontrolled wilderness holds for the controlled social group, the family.

The last chapter of *Little House in the Big Woods* further illustrates the security of home that is so strongly impressed in the book, and this theme of security is reinforced by an informal story Pa tells. Taking Laura and Mary upon his knee, Pa tells them why he came home from hunting without any meat: he had seen a doe and her fawn standing together in the moonlight and he could not bear to shoot them. They represent the family, which Pa would never participate in destroying, and that family was particularly vulnerable in his eyes because they were lacking a male protector. He sees in the deer the only element of wilderness that is in control: the family.

The major emphasis of the tales Pa tells is that safety and security are to be found inside, that danger lurks outside the family threshold, and that Pa, as protector, can control that which is out of control, the wilderness. Pa's use of family members in his stories furthers this emphasis, for the perils encountered in his tales are not far removed from Laura and Mary's arena of experience, making his stories immediate and viable.

Storytelling is a highly formalized ritual, one that develops into a family custom. Other family customs, which may also be highly developed but not so formalized, are also considered within the realm of folklore,[10] but they are not dependent upon time, place, or event: they may have a greater day-to-day continuity than storytelling. Such customs are also evident in *Little House in the Big Woods.*

The most evident of these traditions is Pa's referring to Laura as "little half-pint of sweet cider half drunk up" (*LHBW,* 33), which is shortened to "little half-pint" in *Little House on the Prairie,* the next book in the series. Whether Pa had affectionate nicknames for his other children is not revealed in the books; we know only of this one for Laura.[11]

Other traditions, such as recurring phrases that are particularly enjoyed by the family, may not be overtly identified as folkloric or traditional by the family, but their contexts assure us that they are indeed customary behaviors. Usually Wilder achieves this textual identification of custom by setting off certain lines in quotation, as she does to show that the phrase "saving the bacon" is an intrafamily joke. When the line first appears, Pa has rescued their pig from a bear. After nine paragraphs of narrative, the line occurs, grammatically part of the preceding paragraph but set apart:

Laura was sorry Pa did not get the bear. She liked bear meat so much. Pa was sorry, too, but he said:
"Anyway, I saved the bacon." (*LHBW,* 11)

Later, Pa sees a bear picking up a freshly killed pig and he shoots the bear and brings both it and the pig home. Again, the statement follows narrative and is set off in a separate paragraph:

Pa shot the bear, and there was no way of knowing where the pig came from nor whose pig it was.
"So I just brought home the bacon," Pa said. (*LHBW,* 26)

Both of these uses of "bacon" to refer to a pig is obviously an internal family joke that must have delighted Laura. While this is not an unusual usage, Alan Dundes has observed that many folkloric elements are shared by families who are unaware that other families have the same tradition.[12] Thus, despite the fact that Pa may, indeed, be employing a literal usage of a common idiom, *bringing home the bacon,* to refer to both the pig and his role as breadwinner, its employment in context justifies its designation as a family folkloric element.

Pa also told jokes (*LHBW,* 22). Usually, his jokes were too subtle for Laura and Mary to understand, although they did realize that when Pa was telling a joke, the conversation had elevated to another level. When Pa tells the joke about the man who cut two cat-holes in his door, one for his big cat and one for his small cat, Mary, the older child, comes close to understanding the story, while Laura totally misses the point:

"But why couldn't the little cat—" Mary began.
"Because the big cat wouldn't let it," Laura interrupted. (*LHBW*, 23)

Mary understands why the man's reasoning is illogical but does not grasp the humor, and both escape Laura's perception entirely.

Ma, too, participates in the family folklore. Her contributions are mainly those that are connected with housekeeping, and act as a definition of her role in the family. Her introduction to Laura and Mary of the theory that the moon is made of green cheese (*LHBW*, 190–91) occurs when the children watch her making cheese and taste green (unripened) cheese.

Ma also introduces to Laura and Mary the legend of Jack Frost, who, during long winter nights, draws ice pictures on windows. Ma's success at relaying this folklore is substantiated by Laura's vivid visualization of Jack Frost as a tiny man clad completely in dazzling white and carrying the tools with which he etches designs on the window-glass (*LHBW*, 27). Ma lets Laura and Mary draw circles in the ice on the windows with her thimble, although they never destroy Jack Frost's paintings. This use of the thimble to decorate the window reiterates the domestic orientation of Ma's folklore. Although Jack Frost is a mythic character of the outdoors, it is significant that Laura rejects a gun as part of his costume. Jack Frost is Ma's folkloric property, and Laura models her picturing of him to subscribe to Ma's canon of household propriety—guns are not as much a part of the realm in which Ma operates as are aesthetics. As an artist, Jack Frost does not need to carry a gun; more important to him are the tools of his trade.

Ma's dictum of orderly housekeeping is certainly well known, even today:

> Wash on Monday,
> Iron on Tuesday,
> Mend on Wednesday,
> Churn on Thursday,
> Clean on Friday,
> Bake on Saturday,
> Rest on Sunday.
> (*LHBW*, 29)

Such a system of labor, while it may seem arbitrary at first, was one that produced an efficiently managed home, for all the days of the week were seen as preparations for the most important day: Sunday. What one could do on Sunday was not a matter of personal choice: it was a day that belonged to religion, and religion only. No work could be done, perhaps as much to provide a day of much needed rest as to foster religious reflections. Therefore, the system for home economy was probably less folklore than necessity at the time; today, however, this ordering of weekly chores has moved from one of necessity to one of tradition. [13]

Play activity may also reflect family folklore. In the Ingalls home, the favorite game was "mad dog," in which Pa would muss his hair, crouch on his hands and knees, and, growling, chase Laura and Mary into a corner. Mary would be scared, but Laura would grasp her and pull her over the woodbox to safety (*LHBW*, 36). Such play activity was not simple amusement, but served as a necessary physical exercise during long winter months when outdoor activity was impossible, an outlet for spirited children. The repetition and variation of the game also served to develop their reflexes, so that Laura and Mary would be able to think quickly in the hazardous woods, should they meet a real wild animal. In the safety of their home, they are able to rehearse through role-playing a potentially dangerous situation.

Most of the events in *Little House in the Big Woods*, as in the other books in the series, are accompanied by the sound of Pa's fiddle. Music played a prominent part in the lives of the Ingalls family and served an important function, whether it be soothing excited children, lulling them to sleep, taking their minds off unpleasantries (which is more fully its use in *The Long Winter*), or simply marking an especially pleasant time.

Some songs were reserved for special occasions. On Laura's birthday, Pa plays "Pop Goes the Weasel" as "a special birthday treat" (*LHBW*, 98). It was a favorite song of hers, for it included a game: trying to catch the weasel as Pa made the string pop with his finger.

Pa also uses music to tell stories or to illustrate a point. For instance, he sings "Old Grimes" to show Laura that Ma is a good caretaker, and that the family is in no danger of starving to death, for Ma, unlike Old Grimes's wife, is not stingy when she prepares their food (*LHBW*, 192–93). The song itself has an interesting background; it is sung to the melody of "Auld Lang Syne" and the lyrics have been attributed to *Mother Goose*. [14]

The closing of the book is marked by music, and the song that Pa's fiddle plays carries, in itself, a sense of ending, for it is the traditional New Year's Eve song, "Auld Lang Syne."[15] It is fitting that the song that is used to close the year should also close the book, thus completing the cycle of a year that provides the book's structure.

The tradition of folklore established in *Little House in the Big Woods* recurs frequently in the subsequent volumes in the series. While the family remains the primary source for the transfer of intergenerational knowledge and the initial educational unit, as Laura's world expands beyond her family, the folklore is extended to include other people and even other societies, illustrating the broadening sense of community that results from her increased awareness of the world around her. The respect awarded folklore is evident when Pa heeds the warning of the Indian who advises him about the forthcoming hard winter in *The Long Winter* (*LW,* 61–62). Although this prediction springs from a culture alien to the Ingallses, it is recognized as being based upon experience the Ingalls family does not have, and Pa refuses to dismiss it simply because its source is another society. Pa points out to Ma that "they [the Indians] know some things that we don't" (*LW,* 64). His acceptance of the Indian's warning signifies his trust in this aspect of a Native American "formula" of weather prediction, that every seventh winter is severe, and that every twenty-first winter brings seven months of blizzards.

Hennig Cohen posits that folklore is used in American literature for a variety of reasons: to provide a framework upon which the work may be structured, to enhance or augment characterization, to operate as an element of the plot itself, and, in a broader sense, to clarify or explicate society.[16] In *Little House in the Big Woods,* the society under scrutiny is the Ingalls family. The stories Pa tells create the framework of the book; his stories, as well as the other folkloric elements that appear in the book, identify the roles of the family members within the small society of the family and are integral to the overall plot, creating an atmosphere of warmth and sharing.

Folklore, in its richness and tradition, provides a way of preserving the past and maintaining its vitality so that "now" and "a long time ago" (*LHBW,* 238) remain an inseparable whole. In this case, that "whole" is perhaps the strongest grouping human beings have—the family.

Chapter Three
"It Is Better Farther On"

The *Little House* books examine frontier America in the period immediately following the Homestead Act of 1862. Growing up on the
American frontier and seeing the face of the prairie change with the
rapid encroachment of settlers lured by the promise of "Free land!"
provided Wilder the vibrant backdrop for her narrative. She had wit-
nessed a time in American history that was unique: "I realized that I
had seen and lived it all—all the successive phases of the frontier, first
the frontiersman, then the pioneer, then the farmers and the towns.
Then I understood that in my own life I represented a whole period
of American history."[1]

Wilder used her own family's migration as the basis for her *Little
House* saga, and it is through this centralized focus that the books act
as a supplemental history to the textbook accounts of the westward
movement. Although Wilder may be criticized for halting her narrative before the real-life Ingalls and Wilder families meet what could
be considered their eventual defeat[2] (the Ingalls family moved to town
where her father became a carpenter, and the Wilders left the area
entirely, eventually settling in Missouri), the story told in the *Little
House* books is not that of what happened to Laura Ingalls Wilder and
her family per se. As Laura is the persona Wilder adopted for the central character in her grand epic, so is the Ingalls family a representative family, acting out in a fictionalized format the drama of those
forces that drew people west.

Western expansion, which had been occurring since the nation's
beginnings, was encouraged by the attractions of the Homestead Act.
People streamed west for a variety of reasons; to some it was a chance
to capitalize on the government's offer of "free" land, while to others
the West became a symbol of salvation from a seemingly endless cycle
of poverty. Whatever their motivations, of the thousands that responded to the challenge issued from Washington, only a few realized
that these new, "unsettled" lands would test not only their capabilities for success, but also their ability to survive despite overwhelming

odds, which neither they nor the politicians who framed the Homestead Act (and the subsequent Tree Claim Act of 1873) had considered. Even faced with the evidence that life on the Plains was more arduous than the early advertising promotions had indicated, many were not deterred from pursuing in place after place what had become more than a dream but a personal quest in what William Appleman Williams has called the "mirage of an infinity of second chances."[3] They invested the West with a metaphorical dimension that fit their dreams and in turn shaped the very dreams that had created it.

Throughout the *Little House* series, Laura's father looks to the West for relief. Sometimes it is relief from financial distress, and sometimes it is relief from what he sees as overpopulation. When hunting becomes difficult because game is scarce, or when neighbors crowd too closely, Pa sees the West as a place of escape. Pa's initial interest in the West is based on his concern about the availability of game and his uneasiness with the press of other families in the Big Woods of Wisconsin. He refines his vision of the West by describing it to Ma as they sit inside the cabin in the Big Woods, talking during the winter evenings. The land in the West as he pictures it is quite unlike the Big Woods: it is a flat, grassy, treeless plain, filled with wildlife, and untouched and unspoiled by white settlers (*LHP,* 2).

When the family settles in Indian Territory, Pa assures Ma that this is the country he has been searching for, where the vast sky and seemingly endless stretches of land promise a sense of space that will continue even after settlement (*LHP,* 74).

But he never gets a chance to see Indian Territory settled, for he is the victim of the unreliable information about the West that plagued both settlers and would-be settlers. The distance between Washington, D.C., and the West compounded the problem; news traveled slowly and updates on the land situation were frequently delayed. While the family is moving from the Big Woods, Laura asks Ma whether they are in Indian country. Ma cannot answer, because she does not know exactly where they are, whether they have crossed the line into Kansas. But she is sure that the Indians will leave and the white people will be able to settle there legally. Pa had been told by "a man in Washington" that the area would soon be available for settlement, if it were not already. They have no way of knowing what the current status of the land is, "because Washington was so far away" (*LHP,* 47).

Pa's information was, as the Ingalls family discovers at the end of

Little House on the Prairie, incorrect, or at best incomplete. The land on which they have settled belongs to the Osage Indians and cannot be homesteaded.[4] When Mr. Scott, their neighbor, tells Pa that the settlers will be forced off Indian land by the government, Pa decides to leave before he can "be taken away by the soldiers like an outlaw" (*LHP,* 316). His assertion that he would not have settled there had he not been assured by "some blasted politicians in Washington" (*LHP,* 316) that it was permissible to do so reflects the situation encountered by many would-be settlers in the area who thought their claims secure, but who were instead constrained to leave their homes.[5] It also illustrates how Pa, like other settlers, had acted hastily in moving west, for Ma clearly tells Laura early in *Little House on the Prairie* that Pa does not know whether the area has yet been opened for settlement; he has moved them there on the assurance that it would be, rather than that it is already (*LHP,* 47).

Their next home in the *Little House* books is in Minnesota, on Plum Creek, but here, too, hunting becomes difficult. When he muses to Ma about moving farther west, Ma cuts him off with a reminder that the children must have schooling (*BPC,* 283).

After the family has scarlet fever, and Mary loses her sight, the children's education becomes a secondary consideration. There are day-to-day exigencies that must be faced, and life looks bleak. Not only is hunting difficult, the crops have been bad and the family is in debt for the doctor's bill. Pa sees homesteading as the only chance they have: he is defeated at Plum Creek. Aunt Docia's offer of a job for him in the Dakota Territory seems like a two-fold answer to a prayer. First, it offers immediate financial relief, and second, it offers Pa the opportunity to try homesteading. It means they must move again, but they have no choice: they stay in Plum Creek and face certain failure, or they move and face possible failure—or success. Homesteading was a gamble, but, like many others, the Ingalls family had nothing to gamble with but failure itself.

The wager involved higher stakes than many pioneers realized: making good ("proving up") on a claim was an expensive proposition. While Pa sees the Homestead Act as a way to future economic freedom and prosperity, a neighbor of the Ingalls family, Mrs. McKee, with whom Laura stays as a companion one summer while Mr. McKee works in town, sees the pitfalls of the act in more immediate terms.

In a tirade about the laws governing homesteading, Mrs. McKee notes that they are cruel and dehumanizing, constructed not to allow the individual to free him- or herself from previous financial restrictions, but to force the homesteader into serving a period of humiliating and degrading indentureship to the government. She points out that in setting up the terms of the Homestead Act, the government has been unrealistic. Because farming requires a great deal of initial expense as well as continuing funds to maintain operation, the homesteader must already have enough money to sustain the endeavor, in which case he or she could buy a farm. Alternatively, the homesteader (or the homesteader's family) must be able to earn capital to support the family and the farming enterprise, an ability severely limited by the government's restrictions requiring physical occupation of the claim (*THGY,* 118–19).

Under the provisions of the Homestead Act, land was available for sale as well as for claiming. And in this sense Mrs. McKee was right: the law seemed to allow the poor citizen an equal footing with the wealthy one, but the costs to the farmer of successfully completing a claim were steep enough to prevent the poor from realizing that equality.[6]

The terms of the Homestead Act of 1862 included breaking five of the 160 acres the first year. Before the land could be plowed, it had to be mowed, and that meant buying a mowing machine. The land was, in fact, free,[7] but the machinery was not: new farms required approximately seven hundred dollars' worth of machinery for optimum operation.[8]

In addition to machinery expenses, day-to-day expenses of family living had also to be met. The first year, only hay could be harvested. In the ensuing years, when the capricious midwestern seasons often destroyed the crops with their vicious extremes of heat and cold, and prairie fire, pests, or drought took their toll, supporting the family and at the same time keeping the claim seemed impossible.

There were two solutions to this dilemma. One was that at least one member of the family work elsewhere to earn enough money to keep the claim. If the claim were close enough to town so that the working member or members of the family could walk to and from the job in town, as Pa and Laura did the summer they worked in town, the family could stay together. But often, as in the case of the McKees, the family unit had to be broken apart because the claim was too far away from town, and visits home could be made only on weekends.

In such cases, the structure of the family underwent a transformation. As Wilder notes, the men were occupied with building the foundations of the towns that would support the homesteading ventures financially, while other members of the family were satisfying the requirements of the law and actually doing the homesteading. The daughters and wives were responsible for living in the claim shanties, and the sons did the plowing and planting. The men, who relied upon their families to fulfill the terms of the Homestead Act, were forced to see their own roles in homesteading eroded, reduced to providing financial backing (*LTP*, 49–50).

This passage also directs attention to another aspect of frontier life: settlers on the plains found their dreams of self-sufficiency foiled by pragmatic needs. Lumber, fuel, and other raw materials had to be brought from the East, so that the independence sought by the pioneers was modified by a dependence on the railroad.[9] In *The Long Winter,* when snow prevents the trains from bringing supplies to De Smet, the suddenly isolated community nearly succumbs.

There was more to pioneering, however, than farming and land-ownership. As the pioneers struggled with carving an existence from the harsh environment, they were also developing a society. Some of their cultural activities were vestiges of the activities they knew from the eastern homes; others were their own inventions, specially oriented for this new habitat. These activities reflected the pioneers' desire to make their surroundings true homes in the fledgling communities of the Plains. According to Ray Billington, the search for cultural pastimes marked more than the pioneers' wishes to create amusements and diversions: "This spirit inspired the cultural activities that blossomed at an early stage on every frontier—the literary societies, the debating clubs, the 'thespian groups,' the libraries, the schools, the camp meetings—just as it helped fasten on the pioneers an infinite faith in the future."[10]

The introduction of social functions beyond the family and the development of a popular culture unique to the town's population marked the beginnings of a real community on the frontier. Cultural events became anticipated occurrences that were enjoyed immensely by the settlers. Popular culture serves to identify a community in two ways: the group creates its own culture to affirm its unity first to itself, as a reassurance of the group's continuity and existence as an entity, and second to the world, as a proclamation of that continuity. In return, popular culture aids in the identification of the individual within the group and, like its folkloric relative, modifies behavior to fit within the scope of the group.

The populating of the midwestern territory flourished in the years following the Homestead Act. Very few of the community members had been residents of the area for more than a couple of years; most were recent immigrants from the "East"—which, by their contemporary definition, included almost any area east of the Dakota Territory. Thus the adults arrived with expectations of what the community should do as a community and what functions should be undertaken. Not surprisingly, most community culture was imported from the East, where community standards were already developed and firmly established.

The young people of the budding town often had known no other communities, having grown up on the frontier, or were too young to remember communities in which they had lived as small children, and thus had no information about what community functions were. They had never encountered peer grouping and its associated pressures from outside their own families. For them, the entire concept of a community culture was new, and they were frequently at a loss when it came to behaviors, trends, and what was frequently not-so-friendly peer competition on a social scale.

Adults undertook the responsibility for introducing the young people of the town to social activities, and considered that such activities were not frivolities, but a necessary aspect of creating a community identity. In *Little Town on the Prairie,* the founding of De Smet, in what would eventually be South Dakota, and its rapid growth to an established community is chronicled, with close attention paid to the rise of a unique popular culture.

Like many other frontier settlement children, Laura had limited knowledge about the role of a community. Segregrated by her life as the daughter of a homesteader, she often felt at a disadvantage concerning social functioning. Her father was considered the first settler of De Smet, having arrived when it was still a railroad camp and having remained after the railroad workers had gone, and thus Laura and her sisters can be regarded as the first young settlers of the town.

Much of the popular culture that evolved in De Smet came from the East. For fashion authority, women relied upon *Godey's Lady's Book,* a popular magazine in the East. When Ma is in town buying material to make Mary's dresses for college, she hears from Mrs.

White, who heard from her sister in Iowa, that hoop skirts were returning to fashion in New York (*LTP,* 90–91). Without a *Godey's
Lady's Book* to guide them in tailoring Mary's dresses, they realize
how isolated from national trends and fashion they are. Despite their
seclusion, they are still reliant upon the East for style advice and are
reluctant to develop independent fashionings.

When Ma returns from seeing Mary off to college, she brings Laura
and Carrie presents of autograph books. The girls have no idea what
they are, and Ma must explain them to her daughters. She tells them
that such books are "all the fashion," owned by "the most fashionable
girls in Vinton" (*LTP,* 123), thus establishing that Ma considers such
items not extravagances, but necessary parts of female identity, or at
least the identity she wants her daughters to have; that is, she does
not want them to be disadvantaged by the necessarily limited social
environs of the new prairie town, De Smet.

At school, the other girls also have autograph albums, all except
Nellie Oleson. Nellie, who has recently come from the East and puts
on refined airs about her background and knowledge of trends, scoffs
at her classmates' excitement over the books. Autograph books are
outdated, she loftily explains; in the East, name cards are "all the
rage" (*LTP,* 190). When Ida asks what they are, as Laura had asked
about the autograph albums, Nellie notes scornfully, "Well, of course
you wouldn't know" (*LTP,* 190). The girls find this information un-
settling, for, like the news about the hoop skirts, it underscores their
lack of knowledge about what is going on in the rest of the world.
This uncertainty and insecurity reinforce a dominant fear, for it acts
upon what the young people, like their elders in the community, see
as their greatest weakness: that their physical alienation has also made
them culturally alienated.

A printer in town, Jake, carries the name cards, and Pa says that
Jake is "up-and-coming, bringing out such novelties" (*LTP,* 195),
showing that he, like the other settlers in town, equates knowledge
of the popular trends in the East with business savvy and prosperity
in the new settlement. Pa gives Laura the money to buy some cards,
even though she has not asked for it. In fact, she tries to refuse it,
for money is still tight, but Ma and Pa tell her that they want her to
have what the other girls in town have, reinforcing the already strong
social identity that Laura has with other girls her own age. Fear of
not keeping step with one's peers is a function of adolescence, but one
that is reinforced by fads.

Parties and community activities constituted another form of popular culture. But they also accentuated what the young pioneer settlers perceived as their dreadful lack of knowledge. When the church-sponsored dime sociable is announced, Laura is nonplussed, for she doesn't know—again—what it is. She plans to go with her friend Mary Power, but Laura feels a twinge of doubt, for even with Mary Power she feels "at a slight disadvantage" (*LTP,* 201), because Mary is very fashionable, even to wearing bangs. The night of the sociable, Laura begs permission to cut bangs, which her parents call a "lunatic fringe" (*LTP,* 203–5), but even the fashionable new bangs cannot make Laura feel comfortable at the sociable. She does not know the fine art of small talk and mingling, and feels quite out of place. Afterwards, when she talks it over with her mother, Ma expresses her confidence in the social activity, explaining that she has read that dime sociables are quite popular. Again Ma relies upon information from the East, this time from the Chicago periodical, the *Advance,* and notes that once people become better acquainted with each other, once the community identity is confirmed, such social activities will become more enjoyable.

The town begins to form its own cultural pastimes and includes the young people in the activities. Friday night is reserved for the Literaries, a variety of programs put on by the townspeople that are eagerly attended and discussed. At Thanksgiving the Ladies' Aid Society, which was responsible for the dime sociable, sponsors a New England Supper, which is a resounding success.

The focus returns to the young people as Ben Woodworth celebrates his birthday with a party at his home. Laura receives a gilt-edged invitation, a signal that the culture is becoming more formalized and structured. Carrie, the true child of the prairie, does not even know what a party is like and must ask. Laura, who had been to one on Plum Creek, worries once more about how she should act. Again, her social training is lacking, and although Ma tells her that she has been raised to know how to behave in any circumstance, Laura finds little comfort in her mother's words.

As before, Laura takes solace in the fact that Mary Power is going with her. When the two reach the door of the Woodworth home, Mary hesitates, uncertain whether they should knock or go on in, and Laura finds some relief in Mary's insecurity, which mirrors her own. Inside, all Laura's fears appear to be verified, as she experiences the eternal problem of adolescents in society—her feet seem to have grown startlingly large, and she does not know what to do with her hands. An uneasy silence reigns in the room where the party is, for none of the young people are adept at making small talk. Eventually they are rescued from the trauma by Ben's older brother, Jim, who breaks the silence by making them laugh.

The problem of hoop skirts reappears when Laura, having progressed from a country girl who, at the beginning of *Little Town on the Prairie*, waits until the morning's work is done to rebraid her hair after sleeping on it, to a fashion-conscious young woman by the end of the book, tries to cope with the hoops, which are not at all suited to a climate where the winds blow as strongly or as constantly as they do in the Dakota Territory. As Carrie and Laura walk to school one morning, Carrie observes her older sister twisting to get the hoop skirts down from where they have bunched up around her knees, and notes that she is happy not to have to deal with hoop skirts yet. Although Laura admits that they are "a nuisance," she also explains that "they are stylish, and when you're my age you'll want to be in style" (*LTP,* 273).

Despite the burgeoning popular culture of De Smet, which helped to provide a sense of community, the settlers were susceptible to doubts about their validity as a social group. When Nellie Oleson calls her classmates "You—you—you *ignorant Westerners!*" (*LTP,* 255), the young people are stunned into silence. She has just voiced their unspoken fear, that their isolation on the prairie makes them ignorant.

Nellie's recent contact with the East gives her the upper hand in controlling the youth culture in De Smet. Laura does not plan to go to a religious revival meeting, but when a horrified Nellie exclaims that those who do not attend revivals are "atheists" (*LTP,* 274), Laura realizes she has to go in order to maintain her religious standing in the community and in the eyes of her classmates. As individuals experience the town's socializing influence, they must sacrifice a degree of privacy to establish their public image. Religion is no longer a private matter.

The book ends with the School Exhibition, in which the children must display what they have learned in front of the entire town in recitations and oral examinations. The stock the town has put in the children of De Smet is clear from this final example: so many people show up that the Exhibition must be moved from the schoolhouse to the church.

Laura's part in the Exhibition is the recitation of half the history of the United States; her friend Ida Brown covers the other half. When Laura completes her recitation without error, the town recognizes her accomplishment with thunderous applause. Perhaps the applause is as much for De Smet as it is for Laura, for her perfect recitation is proof that they have done a good job of educating their young people. But more than this, they have created a community; beyond the mandatory church, school, and cemetery that are the standard edifices of a community, they have completed the final step toward permanence: they have established their own identity by encouraging the town's popular culture and seeing it flourish. The process has given a sense of permanence to the settlement and confirmed the pioneers' belief that their activities have a purpose and a future.

The settlers recognized their need for cultural stimulation and personal contact, and they consciously created social groupings as a way of humanizing the often austere prairie. Yet as the pioneer shaped the prairie, so the prairie shaped the pioneer. The curious mingling of the bucolic fantasy of the mythic frontier, in which the land gratefully received the attention of the yeoman farmer, with the actual frontier, in which the land often fought the farmer, produced a person who was capable of retaining his or her dreams while struggling to stay alive, who could plan for the future while considering and reexamining the trappings of civilization. The pioneer was close sighted and farsighted at the same time, and this unique amalgam of vision produced the singular personality of the pioneer. Frederick Jackson Turner, in his landmark essay "The Significance of the Frontier in American History," characterized the pioneer spirit and credited it with contributing to the American identity: "That coarseness and strength combined with acuteness and inquisitiveness; that practical, inventive turn of mind, quick to find expedients; that masterful grasp of material things, lacking in the artistic but powerful to effect great ends; that restless, nervous energy; that dominant individualism, working for good and for evil, and withal that buoyancy and exuberance which comes with freedom—these are the traits of the frontier, or traits called out elsewhere because of the existence of the frontier."[11]

It took a certain kind of person to be a success at pioneering, one who possessed what Wilder identified as the pioneer spirit, one "of humor and cheerfulness no matter what happened. . . . My parents possessed this frontier spirit to a marked degree. . . . They looked forward to better things."[12]

The character of the pioneer is easily romanticized. But the pioneer's actions were not entirely laudable. The frontier desire for "better things" included a rapacious appetite for the land and all that was on it, and Wilder does not ignore or excuse the offenses perpetrated by the pioneer against the land or its original people, the Native Americans.

Laura is introduced to the doctrine of Manifest Destiny in *Little House on the Prairie* when Pa sings one night the legend of the Indian maiden, Alfarata, to her, and Laura asks where the voice of Alfarata went. Ma responds that Alfarata probably went west, because "That's what the Indians do" (*LHP*, 236). When Laura asks why, Pa tries to explain to her that the government will force them to, because white people are settling the country and can claim it. Laura persists with her questioning, and, with the wisdom of youth, arrives at the weak point of the doctrine: if the land belongs to the Indians, will their being forced to give it up not make them angry? Pa does not answer her question but brushes it off by telling her to go to sleep (*LHP*, 236–37). Pa's reluctance—or inability—to explain the logic behind Manifest Destiny illustrates his recognition of its inherent difficulties. Yet it is precisely this doctrine that allows him to satisfy his wanderlust[13] and, while it ultimately does him no good in Indian Territory, that allows him to eventually achieve his dream of earning land through the provisions of the Homestead Act.

The pioneers' prevailing attitude toward Native Americans extends to their attitudes toward the land itself and its resources. As pioneers emptied an area of its native vegetation and animal life and stripped vital minerals from the soil, they moved on, leaving behind them a trail of ecologically depleted lands.[14] The rapidity with which this occurred does not escape Laura's notice, and she does not hesitate to place the blame where it belongs: on the white men who killed the buffalo, which Laura calls "the Indians' cattle" (*SSL*, 62).

As Wilder questions the moral and sociological ramifications of frontiering, she must include Pa and, eventually, herself among those who, in their love for the wilderness, destroyed its very wildness.[15] Early in the series, Pa rejoices in the West as an unplundered paradise in which he can fulfill his dream of self-sufficiency. There seems to be enough game to support them forever; the land will provide for them all, with as much as they can possibly want or need (*LHP*, 49–50).

Yet, by participating in the settling of the western lands, Pa shares the responsibility for the destruction of the land's assets, which drew him there originally. Near the end of *By the Shores of Silver Lake,* he returns empty-handed from a hunting expedition and reports that the geese are no longer stopping at Silver Lake. He speculates that the town, which has changed the geese's natural lake habitat into a noisy cluster of buildings, has driven the birds away permanently (*SSL,* 245). Pa has, with the other settlers in the area, decided the future of what he has always deemed important—hunting—each time he fired a shot or hammered a nail. He has destroyed his own dream.

In *The First Four Years,* Laura experiences homesteading again, this time as an adult. The joyous buoyancy of the preceding books is somewhat subdued as she focuses on the financial aspects of homesteading, measuring her life as a wife and mother by years and growing seasons.

The first year the wheat crop is destroyed by hail. Manly, already deeply in debt for machinery, chattel mortgages on the horses, and building loans on the house, faces more bills for coal and spring seed. He rents out the tree claim, sells the working team of horses, and mortgages the homestead.

The second year the crop is smaller than expected because rainfall has been sparse and the price of wheat is down, but the harvest is enough to pay the interest on the loans and the doctor's bills for their daughter's birth, so the Wilders remain solvent.

The third year a heat wave destroys the wheat, and diphtheria leaves Laura weak and Manly permanently physically impaired. The renter leaves the tree claim, so Manly sells the homestead, and he and Laura move onto the tree claim. As a gamble, they put all their money into a crop the weather will not affect as greatly as it does wheat: they buy sheep.

The fourth year Manly buys two more oxen to finish breaking the sod on his 160 acres. He puts in a seeding of wheat and oats; a dust storm blows it away. He reseeds; drought and hot winds destroy the crop. The sale of the sheep's wool saves them from financial collapse, but they face another problem: the hot winds that destroyed the crops have also killed most of the trees. It is time to prove up and Manly cannot, so he must preempt. After he does, their newborn son dies, and their house burns down, causing them to face the expense of rebuilding it.

The First Four Years ends on a positive note, however. Although

their agricultural ventures have failed, they have been rather successful with animals. Nevertheless, they face a new challenge, for Manly
must have two hundred dollars to prove up on the claim. They face
a fifth year with little in assets but much in optimism: "It would be
a fight to win out in this business of farming, but strangely she felt
her spirit rising for the struggle" (*FFY,* 133).

The *Little House* books are a chronicle of the pioneer experience.
When Wilder said in 1937, during the writing of *By the Shores of
Silver Lake,* that she intended to write "a seven-volume historical
novel for children covering every aspect of the American frontier,"[16]
she implied that the books were to be read as a whole rather than as
individual titles, thus providing not only an historical account but
an historical perspective by one of the participants in the westward
movement. She clarified the veracity of her account of the homesteading years by saying, "Every story in this novel, all the circumstances,
each incident are true. All I have told is true but it is not the whole
truth," and she acknowledged that parts were omitted because they
were unsuitable for children.[17]

What was the "whole truth"? In a letter to her mother, Rose Wilder Lane reminded her, "The truth is a meaning underlying them
[the facts]; you tell the truth by *selecting* the facts which illustrate
it."[18] Wilder's strict point of view and adherence to the truth of experience did not allow her to comment directly upon or interpret the
westering experience from the standpoint of an adult. Nowhere in the
Little House books will one find a wholesale endorsement of frontiering
as a way of life. Frontiering was exhilarating as well as terrifying in
its unpredictability, and the excitement of seeing the prairie in its
natural state permeates Wilder's work. That excitement is, however,
tinged with sorrow, as Laura witnesses the spoiling of the prairie by
the white settlers who kill the buffalo, treat the Indians poorly, and
build towns like De Smet, which Laura calls "a sore on the beautiful,
wild prairie" (*LTP,* 49).

Yet through the seemingly endless battle with the land, through
all the discouragement and disappointment, shines the quality that
was responsible for the westward movement being successful in settling the western lands—the pioneer spirit. What Ray Billington
calls "the heady optimism, the blind faith in the future, [and] the
belief in the inevitability of progress"[19] appears to be the hallmark of
the pioneer creed—a creed Wilder expresses in much the same terms
when Laura considers her future as the wife of a farmer: "The incur-

able optimism of the farmer who throws his seed on the ground every spring, betting it and his time against the elements, seemed inextricably to blend with the creed of her pioneer forefathers that 'it is better farther on'—only instead of farther on in space, it was farther on in time, over the horizon of the years ahead instead of the far horizon of the west" (*FFY*, 133–34).

Chapter Four

The Face under the Sunbonnet

The American frontier gave the United States one of its first abiding images of women as a part of a historical movement or era. Her face often symbolically shaded with a sunbonnet, the pioneer woman has intrigued writers, artists, and historians, who have interpreted not only her appearance but her experiences in a variety of ways. In the novels of Hamlin Garland are grim portrayals of women stripped of their femininity by the hardships of frontier life, while the women in Ole Rölvaag's work are mentally ravaged by their experiences. Harvey Dunn painted portraits of strong, capable women who seemed to embody the Dakota landscape, and in W. H. D. Koerner's well-known painting, "Madonna of the Prairie," a young woman sits in the seat of a Conestoga wagon, her delicate hands resting on the reins, while the bowed wagon cover frames her face like a halo. Under the metaphorical sunbonnet were a variety of visages, yet none of them can be said to represent all frontier women, for the women who came west brought with them their own personalities and expectations, both of which were challenged by this new frontier.

Because most of the characters in the *Little House* books are female, and because the books are based upon actual people and events in Wilder's life, the *Little House* series provides a unique look at the girls and women who settled in the West, particularly those who came with their families.[1] For some, the experience was devastating; for others, it was simply another facet of married life; for still others, it was an exciting challenge.

Many of the women who accompanied their husbands west had spent their entire lives in the East, while others, like Ma, had lived on its outer fringes, near the frontier although not actually close enough to feel its influence. Both were raised with the generally accepted norms of the traditional eastern life-style. The westward movement tested this life-style, one in which families settled in an area and stayed for generations. As Julie Roy Jeffrey notes in *Frontier Women: The Trans-Mississippi West, 1840–1880,* "emigration forced women to modify normal behavioral patterns. . . . [T]he frontier, which for most women began as soon as they left home and friends, challenged conventional sex roles and accepted modes of behavior."[2] With the new life-style demanded in the West, the rules women had learned to live by—and to place their trust in—were altered. Thus the frontier woman had no behavioral guides for dealing with her transplanting to another location. She was compelled to formulate her own answers from what were the primary contemporary texts of socialization for women: the Bible and women's magazines, especially *Godey's Lady's Book.*

The Bible supplied spiritual guidance, but *Godey's Lady's Book* brought more specific help to the woman confronting emigration. *Godey's* contained reviews of guide-books to the West, but the guide-books themselves were often of dubious value to the westering woman, for they were generally male oriented.[3] For the woman who was already west, *Godey's* provided a connection with what was still the place of fashion authority, the East, and strengthened this link by operating a mail-order service through which women could order otherwise unavailable fashion trimmings.[4] *Godey's* was therefore able to establish itself as more than a source of diverting or entertaining reading: it became a vital source of continuity between the two life-styles. Women looked to the magazine for assistance not only during the transition from East to West, but as a way of maintaining cultural ties between the two regions once they were west. For example, when Ma makes Mary's clothes for her college trip, she mourns the lack of *Godey's* as a guide for current style (*LTP,* 90–91).

In an attempt to make the transition to the West easier, women often brought relics of their past with them, reminders of a life-style that had once been theirs. Because space in the covered wagon was at a premium, such symbols had to be small and were often knick-knacks.[5] Ma's memento is the china shepherdess, an image that permeates the *Little House* books with her essence. For Ma, the shepherdess represents home. The ceremonial placing of the shepherdess on the mantel, or later on the whatnot, signifies Ma's acceptance of the quarters as "home." It is not displayed when the home is temporary. When the family moves into the surveyors' house at Silver Lake, Pa asks Ma where the china shepherdess is, and she tells him that she has not unpacked it because the surveyors' house is not their permanent, and thus true, home (*SSL,* 74).

The shepherdess is Ma's touch of refinement in the rough wilderness. When Pa finishes putting down the puncheon floor in Kansas, Ma adds her touches, her elements of civilization—a red-checkered tablecloth and the china shepherdess (*LHP,* 129). Perhaps the china shepherdess represents a settling and merging of the expectations of frontier life and the romanticized dream of its possibilities. It is a sustaining image of an ideal—the female version of the mythic yeoman farmer.

The china shepherdess also represents a continuity of the past with the present, an image of constancy in an unstable territory. Each time the figurine is placed with honor in the house, Wilder notes that it has not changed, as she does in *On the Banks of Plum Creek,* when she observes that the rough travel in the covered wagon from Wisconsin to Kansas and then to Minnesota has not taken its toll on the little china statue: "She was not broken. She was not nicked nor even scratched. She was the same little shepherdess, smiling the same smile" (*BPC,* 122–23). This passage shows the strongest identification of Ma with the china shepherdess: just as the figurine is "not broken, . . . nicked or even scratched" by her experience, neither is Ma. And to further define this identification, no one but Ma is allowed to touch the figurine (*LHP,* 118; *BPC,* 315). It is her personal link with her past, a symbol of order, tranquillity, and endurance, the very qualities Ma must bring to her new environment to provide the stability her family needs.

The frontier introduced not only new experiences but new fears. Most of the women had never before been that alone, that isolated. In addition to continuing threats from the environment, such as wild animals and severe weather, a culturally alien situation confronted them. Another society, quite unlike their own, was sharing the same countryside, and the pioneer women did not know what this society's civilization was like. They were unacquainted with Indian customs and conventions, and being unable to communicate with them except by the most basic of signals undoubtedly increased the white women's frustration and apprehension.

Often the man of the house was not at home when the Indians dropped by, and his absence during such stressful times underscored the frontier woman's lack of reassurance, which social guidelines had hitherto provided. She had to deal outside her socially assigned role.

Whereas the man had previously been totally accountable for the family's protection, suddenly the woman was faced with a great deal of that responsibility. The first time Ma meets any Indians, Pa is gone, and she is alone with the children (*LHP*, 132–46). The fear that she experiences is a basic one, stemming from a quite natural anxiety about the hazard of confronting any stranger alone, particularly when that meeting occurs at her home with her children present. This anxiety is compounded by her recognition of cultural differences: she does not know what to expect. Her reaction is based upon an instinctive fear of the unknown, and she responds cautiously, allowing the visitors to determine the course of the meeting.

Amplifying women's fears were stories of clashes between the two cultures, some real, many existing only in the minds of writers who capitalized on the current popularity of the Indian as a literary figure. Disputes between Indians and white settlers undoubtedly added an aura of justification to those stories, which represented the Indian as a savage adversary, thus increasing the women's anxiety about their strange new environment. When Mrs. Scott tries to tell Ma about a massacre, Ma stops her, reminding her that the children can hear (*LHP*, 211–12). Ma's reluctance to let Mrs. Scott continue her recounting of the events may have been motivated not only by the fact that the children can hear, but by the fact that she does not want to reinforce her own anxiety.

Ma's dislike of the Indians is stressed in the *Little House* books, usually in contrast to Pa's reserved judgment, but Wilder makes it clear that Ma's dislike stems from fear. To Ma, the Indians are a physical representation of the very nature of the prairie: she does not know the limits of either. She has experienced some of the tremendous power the prairie has over the settlers, and she does not trust it. This, combined with the stories she has heard about the Indians, makes her fear them and their capability in this environment, which has her at a disadvantage. The Indians are in control of the same surroundings in which she must act with cautious reserve.

It is important to recognize that Pa meets Indians in entirely different situations than Ma, and the interactions he has are of quite a different sort. It is he who meets Soldat du Chêne, the Osage who dissuades the tribes on Lower Reserve from attacking the white settlers, and it is he who meets, in town at the store where many other men are present, the lone Indian who warns the settlers about the impending long winter. The Indians he encounters are more than just

friendly; he owes his family's survival to them, whereas the circumstances under which Ma meets them cause her to fear for her family's
survival.

The one time Pa is at home when an Indian stops by, they exchange greetings before the Indian dismounts from his horse. The Indian shares an uneasy and silent meal with the Ingalls family, and
still Pa does not experience the feeling of invasion that Ma does when
an Indian appears beside her in the house, and he dismisses her worries (*LHP*, 229).

Pa does not seem to understand that Ma's fears are not only for the
personal safety of herself and her family, but for her privacy and the
future of her family's sustenance. When she gives food to the Indians,
she is confronting what many frontier women faced—the reminder
that the white people's place on the frontier was tenuous, and surren-
dering the family's provisions, which might mean the difference between life and death, reinforced an already present fear that food—or
rather the lack of it—might be their eventual undoing.[6]

Women confronted other perils on the frontier, and one of the major dangers they faced was themselves. Forced to leave behind them
a generations-old life-style, women encountered new challenges, and
creativeness was often their only recourse against desperation so in-
tense it sometimes led to insanity. Often this creativity was self-
expressive, as with those women who kept journals of their experiences, while for other women it was channeled into practical forms,
frequently home-oriented in focus and scope.

Ma's creative power marks her personality as one of great ingenu-
ity. She improvises both games and food to keep her family's minds
off pressing problems: for instance, when the blackbirds eat almost
all the corn the Ingalls family has been planning on for income, she
saves what is left by making parched corn for winter, and she fries
some of the blackbirds and makes others into a pie (*LTP*, 102–6).
This is more than economy, or "making do." Ma is expressing her
creativity in the sphere where she is most expert: the home. The
bleakest of times seems to stimulate her creativity. Ma's motto is
"There's no great loss without some small gain" (*LTP*, 102). Although she is referring to physical gain, her motto can be applied to
mental gain: by frying the blackbirds, she is transforming them from
agents of destruction (destroyers of the crop) to agents of support
(food). There is a triumph of justice—what eats their food becomes
their food, and from the loss is salvaged a gain.

When Laura leaves De Smet to teach, she meets a woman who has not adapted well to the frontier, Mrs. Brewster, at whose house Laura stays. Mrs. Brewster intensely hates living on the claim and does not disguise her feelings, alternating sullen silences with loud complaints about her environment. Her complaints extend to having to house Laura, and one scene in particular points out the problem faced by many frontier women. As Mrs. Brewster rails against Laura's presence, Laura lies in her bed and cannot help overhearing. She realizes that she is not really the source of Mrs. Brewster's displeasure, although Laura does not truly understand why Mrs. Brewster is upset: she attributes Mrs. Brewster's outburst to selfishness, without acknowledging the stress the woman is experiencing. Instead, Laura identifies with Mr. Brewster, interpreting his silence as stoic forbearance. The next morning, she tells herself, "I have only to get through one day at a time" (*THGY*, 23).

Laura also does not understand that she and Mrs. Brewster have, during the weeks they share a house, the same problem. Like Laura, Mrs. Brewster has no place else to go, and, like Laura, she can hope only to get through one day at a time. What Laura does have that Mrs. Brewster does not is the knowledge that this dreadful experience will soon be over because it is, for Laura, a temporary situation, whereas Mrs. Brewster sees her life continuing in this same hopeless pattern until she dies.

Without an outlet for her personal needs, and without any apparent recognition of whatever sacrifices she has made for this difficult life-style, Mrs. Brewster eventually gives way under this strain, and Laura witnesses the eruption (*THGY*, 64–66). Laura has just gone to sleep when she is awakened by a scream. Through a gap in the curtains she can see Mrs. Brewster, holding a butcher knife over Mr. Brewster. Mrs. Brewster wants to go home so badly that she has been driven to this desperate action of threatening her husband. Mr. Brewster manages to talk his wife into returning the knife to the kitchen, but the event is indicative of the extent to which the pressures of frontier living have driven her.

Mrs. Brewster is not a willing pioneer, and the sacrifices she has been asked to make are not satisfied by her new life. Although her husband notes that all he has in the world is the claim, he neglects the fact that she has no more than he does. Mrs. Brewster's explosive anger comes from frustration at the limitations placed on her by this life: the desolation, the constant struggle with living conditions and

the environment, the entire tenuousness of their existence—the bleak-
ness of her own future on the frontier. For her, the West does not
represent freedom but imprisonment; there is no growth, only restriction, and she cannot consider it her home.

The latter half of the 1800s marked a crucial time in the developing recognition of the equality of women in American society: they
were confronting what seemed to be an opportunity for freedom—the
right to vote. The suffrage movement, although its roots were in the
East, appeared to garner its earliest support from the new West, for
in 1869 Wyoming became the first state to extend the right to vote
to women, and Utah followed suit in 1870.

The struggle for suffrage in South Dakota began in 1872 while the
state was still a part of the Dakota Territory. Preceding statehood in
1889, three major campaigns were waged: in 1872, a bill granting
women the full franchise was passed by one house but vetoed by the
other; the 1879 legislative session passed a bill allowing women to
vote in school elections; and in 1885, the year Laura Ingalls married
Almanzo Wilder, women in the Dakota Territory were given the
right to vote in all elections until the governor vetoed the bill shortly
after its passage by both houses.[7]

The emphasis on female suffrage that year narrowed the definition
of women's rights to the single issue of the vote. When Almanzo asks
Laura if she is "for woman's rights," Laura says, "No . . . I do not
want to vote" (*THGY*, 269). But she does take a stand on another
issue—the use of the word *obey* in the wedding ceremony. Almanzo
agrees with her that she should not use it, and he has apparently already spoken to the minister about it, for he tells Laura that the minister does not believe in using *obey* in the ceremony either. Almanzo's
reasoning behind his not supporting the usage in the wedding ceremony illustrates his acceptance of the equality of women: "I never
knew one [woman] that did it, nor any decent man that wanted her
to" (*THGY*, 269).

Laura objects to the use of the word *obey* in the wedding ceremony
because she feels it prevents her from exercising her own judgment,
but other women on the frontier found that the use of the word violated the relationship between husband and wife that had grown up
in the new West, as both of them struggled in a partnership to make
their life together successful.[8]

Often such a partnership required a redefinition of traditional roles
into a simple division of labor to achieve a common goal.[9] It is pre-

cisely this division of roles that forces Ma into an uncomfortable compromise concerning Laura's participation in physical labor on the claim. Because there are no sons in the Ingalls family, Ma must allow Laura to abandon her assigned role as a female so that the necessary labor on the claim can be accomplished. When the hay must be stacked and there is no money to hire men, Ma reluctantly agrees that Laura can help. Curiously, one of Ma's objections to Laura's doing farm labor is that it is un-American. Ma equates women doing field work with foreigners. She believes that as Americans, she and her daughters are "above doing men's work" (*LW,* 4).

Like other women of her time Ma had been raised on school texts that celebrated ladylike behavior. The effects of this upbringing upon Ma's standards of female propriety are evident when she speaks to Laura before Laura and Pa leave their home to spend an afternoon watching the men build the railroad through Silver Lake. Ladies, she reminds Laura, do not mingle with laborers, who have rough manners and language; women's ways should be gentle, their speech restrained, and they should never draw attention to themselves. She also cautions Laura not to take her cousin Lena with her, for Lena has what Ma considers to be a major flaw: she is "boisterous." Ma clearly faults Docia, Lena's mother, for Lena's exuberance; she tells Laura that Docia has failed to "curb" her daughter (*SSL,* 95–96). Obviously, Ma's criterion for acceptable female behavior includes a subduing of innate human response.

Lena represents unbridled freedom, and it is while the Ingallses stay with Lena's family that Laura has her most rambunctious moments. One of them occurs after a very sobering experience, and the sharp contrast illuminates the dual nature still pressed upon young women growing up on the prairie. Lena and Laura pick up Aunt Docia's laundry at a claim shanty where a tired, unkempt woman excuses her appearance with the news that her daughter has been married the day before. She was only thirteen, a bit older than Laura and a year younger than Lena. It makes them realize how quickly their childhood is ending, and in what is almost a celebration of childhood, they spend the rest of the afternoon in the wild abandon of play, racing across the prairie on galloping ponies (*SSL,* 49–55).

Despite Lena's image as a girl free of restraints, she is a young woman who, rather than being midway between the two worlds of childhood and womanhood, actually lives primarily in one and vacates it to live in the other as need or opportunity dictates. She and her mother cook and wash dishes for the forty-six men of the Silver Lake camp; they work from sunrise until late into night (*SSL*, 46). When she has the chance to move from the work of the woman's world to the play of the child's, she does so almost fiercely, as if to protect the latter from the former and to conserve whatever liberty she has left.

Laura's initiation into the ways of genteel womanhood is continued into her teens, as does her struggle to adapt to the confining standards of nineteenth-century femininity. When Laura speaks too loudly, Ma reminds her that she must always behave like a lady, and that part of a ladylike mien includes not just being careful about what one says, but controlling the manner in which one speaks (*LTP*, 97).

Ma's views on proper female activity are often at odds with Laura's. One of their major points of contention is Laura's sunbonnet. Ma wants Laura to wear a sunbonnet whenever she is outside, but Laura hates the way it prevents her from seeing all around her. When Laura is older, she must wear corsets, and although Ma urges Laura to wear her corsets to bed, Laura resists the confining bands. Of course Laura has to learn how to sew, and Ma encourages her, but Laura finds needlework tedious and frustrating. What Ma wants for Laura is the accepted female role, one of restriction. By rejecting the sunbonnet Laura rejects the pioneer symbol of adult womanhood. The sunbonnet, like blinders on a horse, restricts her vision, the corset restricts her breathing, and the tedious hours of sewing restrict her freedom. Laura wants that freedom.

Laura's desire for the freedom offered by the West is a major theme of the *Little House* books. That this desire is seen by Wilder as being in contraposition to the usual standards for women on the frontier is made apparent by the careful identification of her longings with her father's: other women in the series do not express the same identification with the frontier that Laura does. For Laura and Pa, the West stands as an image of freedom, the antithesis of civilization, in which they feel trapped and confined. For both of them, it remains a dream just out of reach, visible yet lying beyond their immediate grasp. Their conception of the West ties them together, for they find a sympathy and an empathy for each other's dreams that those around them do not share or understand. Laura dreads being enclosed in a classroom all day where she is entrapped in one of the centers of the civilization she longs to escape—the school (*THGY*, 139).

Laura's symbols of self-identification are those of the frontier's wildness. After she leaves the Big Woods, her preferences switch: instead of favoring the inner (safe) over the outer (unsafe), she is drawn to the outer and rejects the inner. This is the source of her statement to Pa that she prefers wolves to cattle despite Pa's reminder that the latter are "more useful" (*BPC,* 79). As the series progresses, Laura appropriates more symbols, the strongest of which are Indians and ponies. She initially hesitates before accepting them, as she does with the wolves, for she recognizes in them a capacity for ferocity—a savagery that is echoed in the prairie, Laura's major symbol of self-identification.

Ma's symbols of self-identification are those of home: the china shepherdess and the red-checkered tablecloth. Unlike Laura, Ma prefers the inner to the outer, and her symbolism reflects this.

The differences in the ways Laura and Ma perceive their environment is evident in their approaches to the dugout house at Plum Creek. Ma says of it, "It is all so tame and peaceful. . . . I haven't felt so safe and at rest since I don't know when," while Laura "would rather sleep outdoors, even if she heard wolves, than be so safe in this house dug under the ground" (*BPC,* 17).

The medium of the Ingalls family supplies a context for examining the different ways females perceived their new environment: the contrast between Ma and Laura and their reactions to the frontier as they face it for the first time is a basic contrast of the adult transplanted to the frontier and the child planted in the frontier.

The pioneer women's behavior was perhaps less a result of the frontier influence as of the family environment and relationships that existed before emigration to the West. Yet, as Elizabeth Hampsten points out, the immediate environment of the living quarters was not without its own impact.[10] Sod houses were impossible to keep clean and tended to collapse, and claim shanties were generally quite small and flimsy because they were built quickly as temporary housing to satisfy the law and prevent claim jumping. Close quarters, particularly during a lengthy winter, had an effect on all family members. The family itself could be strengthened or ripped apart by confinement and the resulting lack of privacy. Tempers flare during *The Long Winter;* even the equanimous Ma snaps at Pa, an indication of the stress the family is under.

Weather, however, was not the only restraint. Children, who were permitted by virtue of their age to romp about the prairie, probably found the frontier environment less restricting than did adult women who felt constrained by behavioral training to limit both their motions and their sphere of activity to the home.

While Ma despaired of the often crude living conditions on the prairie, Laura reveled in them. This was, apparently, not uncommon among the children of the frontier, who found great happiness in what their mothers frequently despaired. Although women's diaries display a variety of interpretations of the new frontier,[11] one historian notes:

An interesting contrast [to the diaries of women who moved to the frontier as adults] is provided by the memoirs of women who discovered the West as children or young girls, or who were born there. They generally looked back to that time of their life with great pleasure and tell with much zest of the freedom, the fascinating discoveries, the joys of life close to nature. Having no experience of a different life, they were not constantly making comparisons and regretting past conditions. Whereas many of the testimonies written by women who moved to the western states in their mature life and had to adjust to primitive conditions would constitute excellent material for a study of the various forms human unhappiness can take, the accounts of childhoods spent in the West are refreshing and full of joy.[12]

The excitement of exploration and discovery in a land that never was what it seemed to be—an apparently flat prairie that held such secrets as moonpaths leading to silver-furred sentinel wolves and buffalo wallows carpeted with violets—appeals to Laura, but not to Ma. Their reactions to the unpredictability of pioneer life perhaps indicate the greatest difference between Laura and Ma. For Laura it is a positive response; for Ma it is negative. Laura enjoys the settling, while Ma enjoys the settled.

Both Laura and Ma can be seen as representing typical frontier women, for the frontier was settled by both types, by both generations. Their reactions depended strongly upon their early environment: for the frontier woman like Ma, the prairie was competing with a previous home, whereas for the frontier child like Laura, the prairie was her home. As Laura explained to Almanzo, "I have always lived in little houses. I like them" (*THGY*, 215).

Chapter Five

Expression of Growth through Language and Experience

The theme of growth is important in any work of fiction, but it is especially significant in those written for children. The protagonist of a children's book must, within the span of the work, develop in character and maturity, resulting in movement from naiveté to knowledge through experience. The *Little House* books are unique in the scope of adult or children's literature, for they provide a look at this growth, from the dual viewpoint of the child (Laura) and the adult (Wilder).

Growth in children's literature may result from the introduction of factors from outside the child's world, or it may result from the child's being forced into another world. The latter is the case in the early *Little House* books, in which Laura is taken from the security of the "little house in the Big Woods" into the strangeness of the open prairie. This departure from security and an accepted easy comfort forces her to undergo cultural redefinition, and she suffers a form of shock—hesitancy and withdrawal—at first, but from this shock comes growth—and emotional survival and development.

Because the *Little House* books encompass Laura's life from her early childhood to her fourth year of marriage, her emotional growth must be shown subtly so that the reader feels that Laura is maturing rather than being told that she is.[1] In addition to increasing the reading difficulty of each book as the series proceeds, thus altering the "voice" of the main character to conform with her age, Wilder achieves this sense of change in three ways: by having Laura begin to see the world in terms of integration rather than segregation, by manipulating the image of the stars, and by developing Laura's recognition of language.

Laura's survival results from her evolving ability to integrate new experiences with prior knowledge. While she is not consciously aware of this evidence of maturation and rarely shows an immediate recognition of this growth, a survey of the *Little House* series reveals such development. The shift in her perception of experience from a dichotomous ordering of known/unknown and safe/unsafe to an integrated expression is revealed by the change in the way she perceives her environment.

Laura's way of seeing, and thus defining, her environment details her growth. In *Little House in the Big Woods,* her main concern is security, and that security is her home. Prevalent words used to describe it are "safe," "snug," and "cosy"—words of closure and defense against both the known and the unknown perils the world outside her home holds. The elements of snow and wind belong to the outer world, but Laura sees them as desiring to be part of the inner world. The snow hugs the sides of the little house and the wind "cries" because it cannot be inside where all is snug, including Laura (*LHBW,* 44). Inside is preferable to outside in the young Laura's eyes, and to her, it is only natural that the outer elements would want to be part of the inside. The house is a refuge for Laura, a sanctuary against what she does not know or understand. The contrast between the inner and outer worlds is a dichotomy expressed throughout *Little House in the Big Woods* and part of *Little House on the Prairie.*[2] It becomes resolved only through an integration of knowledge and experience.

Laura sees the outer world as threatening and feels vulnerable in it. She depends upon Pa and Jack the dog to protect her from it. They act as intermediaries between the outer world (unknown and unsafe) and the inner world (known and safe). Jack guards the door of their home, and Pa's gun is placed over the door where it will be readily available if danger should threaten any of the little house's inhabitants (*LHBW,* 3). Pa and Jack are the only characters in *Little House in the Big Woods* who are capable in both the inner and outer worlds; to them Laura entrusts her survival.

The descriptive passages of *Little House in the Big Woods* reinforce the theme of the inner world as security. The sights and smells of the full attic that Wilder describes are, on the primary level, indicative of a hunger-free Wisconsin winter. They represent physical survival. On the secondary level, they indicate security against the outside: all that the family needs is inside, where Laura can see and smell it. The foodstores in the attic are proof of the family's ensured survival, tangible evidence that they are safe, inside the cabin walls. When Laura and Mary play in the attic, Wilder's word choice again emphasizes

Laura's distinction between the inner and the outer worlds. The contrast of the words "cold and lonesome" to describe the howling of the wind with the "snug and cosy" atmosphere of the attic emphasizes the dual ordering of the world as a child sees it (*LHBW,* 20). For the young child, the gradations of experience between polar extremities have not been introduced: everything is either one way or another, with no shading between the two possibilities.

As *Little House in the Big Woods* closes, Laura has not yet had to leave her home. Her concept of the world has not been challenged. The first seventy pages of *Little House on the Prairie,* the second book in the series, describe in detail her being forced to examine a larger part of the world than she has before acknowledged as being part of her own. In fact, she does not truly know that it exists. It is the prairie. The contrast between the spaciousness of the prairie and the close neighborhoods of the Big Woods is great, and at first she does not like what she sees. To her, the prairie is a void, and the family's covered wagon is the only token of life that she sees. She does not feel as threatened as she would if she were alone on the prairie, however, because she has Jack and Pa to act as her guardians (*LHP,* 7). On the prairie, Pa and Jack retain their roles as protectors, which Laura has assigned them in *Little House in the Big Woods.*

Like most young children, Laura has an egocentric view of the universe, which Jean Piaget attributes to the child's inability to separate him- or herself from the surrounding world.[3] Wherever Laura happens to be is the middle of the world. Visual evidence seems to support her belief, for she stands exactly between two horizons, no matter where she goes:

In a perfect circle the sky curved down to the level land, and the wagon was in the circle's exact middle. . . .

Next day the land was the same, the sky was the same, the circle did not change. (*LHP,* 13)

Laura and her family are literally the center of her world, no matter where they go or how her world may be transformed by a new environs.

Laura's perspective on her environment is forced to undergo a change, for her surroundings offer a new visual prespective: she can see more than she could before. The sky seems bigger, the land larger, and suddenly Laura and her family seem smaller: "In all that space of land and sky stood the lonely, small, covered wagon. And close to it sat Pa and Ma and Laura and Mary and Baby Carrie, eating their breakfasts" (*LHP,* 41). The careful enumeration of the members of the Ingalls family reflects Laura's incipient ability to place people and things in a rudimentary cosmology, and to realize that all the necessary components of her safety are there—her family (home) is there, so she is secure. The narrowing of the field of vision from land and sky to the covered wagon to each member of the Ingalls family to the detail of eating breakfast is a further reassurance for her that life is continuing as it should, and that she is still safe, even in this unknown world.

Laura is still awed, however, by the comprehension of how small she is in comparison to the world. She does not yet know where, if anywhere, the world ends. She is unable even to imagine what happens or what exists beyond her field of vision. When Pa leaves the camp to go hunting, she observes the effect of perspective and concludes that once he is gone from her sight, he has vanished not only visually but physically, leaving the prairie quite empty (*LHP,* 42). Laura does not understand that simply because Pa has disappeared, the prairie is not empty—for she does not know how far the prairie world extends, and cannot judge beyond empirical evidence. She sees nothing, so the prairie must be empty.

As Laura begins to know the prairie, her attitude changes, and a reconciliation of the previously known world and this new world creates one world for Laura. Nevertheless, she still limits her definition of the world to what she has experienced, and the focus is still self-centered: she considers the horizon to be "the very edge of the world" (*LHP,* 48).

Laura's education in the "world" is furthered by her acquaintance with their new neighbor, Mr. Edwards. He is unlike anyone Laura had met in the Big Woods, and he challenges her conception of how the world is peopled, for she has, up to this point, seen the prairie as un-peopled. Her first knowledge of someone who is not a relative, as her neighbors in the Big Woods were, helps her structure her ideas about the unknown. She likes Mr. Edwards, who comes out of the prairie, so the prairie must be capable of producing other interesting people and adventures. When Mr. Edwards leaves, the prairie is no longer an "empty endless land" (*LHP,* 26) but "a shadowy mellowness" (*LHP,* 69). Laura has achieved a harmonious understanding of the prairie.

As Laura's knowledge of the world has changed, so has her knowledge of herself and her position in the world. The last lines of each of the first two books in the series express the tremendous change in Laura's perception of the world and of herself in the world. It is a change in visual perception and, concurrently, in mental perception forced by the prairie. In *Little House in the Big Woods,* the focus is on the home and the immediate moment, for her world is still self-centered and present-centered, and her favored environment is a closed one.

But in *Little House on the Prairie,* the final image is one of the openness of the prairie, of travel and wandering, and the promise and lure of freedom. Her imagination has grown enough for her to equate and understand the kinship of the land and the sea: the waves of grasses are very much like the waves of the sea, and both are filled with potential for adventure and exploration. Her universe, with her acceptance of the prairie world, has expanded to include even that which she does not know and has not seen. The growth from the cosy closed scene of *Little House in the Big Woods* to the open, expansive scene of *Little House on the Prairie* echoes that expansion and that vision.

The changing image of the stars also illustrates Laura's growth. The stars, which are a part of another sphere, are a consistent image Wilder uses to illustrate Laura's reconciliation with the alien realm of the prairie. The development of the image details Laura's evolving ability to assess perspective. Because they are a predominant image only in *Little House on the Prairie* and *These Happy Golden Years,* the stars provide a means of evaluating the contrast between Laura's ability as a child and as an adult to interpret the universe. What the stars symbolize changes: the naive young Laura sees them quite differently from the way the sophisticated adult Laura does.

In *Little House in the Big Woods,* Laura sees the stars as part of the outer world, and, through her dichotomous arranging of the world into outer/inner and negative/positive, the stars suffer in comparison to an element of the inner world: when Laura goes with Ma to milk Sukey at night, she perceives the light from the lantern Ma carries as being brighter and warmer than the stars (*LHBW,* 104).

Early in *Little House on the Prairie,* Laura cannot comprehend the seemingly distorted perspective that the openness of the prairie affords her, and her interpretation of the stars exhibits her difficulty in evaluating the size and distance of things on the prairie; the stars, which are supposed to be far away, have never seemed so enormous nor so close to her, close enough that they seem nearly within reach (*LHP,* 13). The camp fire, which is much larger than the lantern Ma carried in the Big Woods, should also be brighter and thus outshine the stars. Instead, its power is faint compared to that of the stars, thus challenging her conception of the home (the camp fire) as having domination over the outer world (the stars).

Laura struggles to understand this new perspective, and again she depends upon Pa to act as her intermediary. At one point, as she is drifting off to sleep, she imagines that the stars hang from the sky by threads, and they seem so large and close that she thinks Pa can pluck one from the sky for her (*LHP,* 37). Laura is attempting to integrate the stars into her realm of experience by linking them with the inside world: "thread" is something that belongs in the house, and so the large star is not placed in the sky by some mysterious, unknown force—it is, instead, suspended there by something Laura can identify, an element of safety: it is the same thread that holds her buttons on her dress.

As Laura's perceptions and conceptions of the world are challenged, images begin to mix, the abstract with the concrete, the metaphysical with the physical, echoing her confused apprehension of her environment. She believes she hears music in the prairie night air, and attributes part of it to the stars (*LHP,* 50–51).

When the Ingalls family lives in a settled area, the stars become allied with a symbol of civilization, the church, but the association is still musical. While Laura and her family are riding to church on Christmas Eve, the new churchbell rings across the prairie, and Laura equates the sound with the melody of the stars (*BPC,* 249).

This mingling of the stars and music in *Little House on the Prairie* and *On the Banks of Plum Creek* is repeated in *These Happy Golden Years,* providing a full contrast between the imaginal perceptions of the child and the adult. In the later book the stars become a symbol of unification as they are associated with Laura's courtship and marriage. When Laura rides home from singing school with Almanzo Wilder, she looks at the stars again and sees them differently. This time they do not produce music themselves; instead, Laura sings for them, first "In the starlight," (*THGY,* 207) and later, "The heavens declare the glory of God . . ." (*THGY,* 213). When Almanzo asks her to sing "the starlight song," she finishes the song she had begun earlier: "In the starlight, in the starlight, / We will wander gay and

free . . ." (*THGY,* 213–14). Holding her hand, "white in the starlight" (*THGY,* 214), Almanzo asks her to marry him. What had
been a symbol of uncertainty becomes a symbol of solidity.

Laura interprets the songs of the stars one final time when she
sings: "The stars are rolling in the sky, / The earth rolls on
below. . . ." The song, which compares the revolving stars and earth
to the turning wheels below, sums up the essence of the fully developed image of the stars and reflects her integration of the spiritual
and the physical aspects of the world, the culmination of a lifetime
of assessing experience as the stars and the earth rotate in unison
(*THGY,* 238).

The ways in which Laura discovers the intricacies of language and,
later, its deficiencies, further illustrate her maturation. The evolution
of her language discovery is complicated by her having to "see out
loud" for her blind sister, thus burdening the already precarious relationship Laura has with words. From her initial difficulties in understanding linguistic subtleties in *Little House in the Big Woods* to her
caution in approaching the language of her marriage vows in *These
Happy Golden Years,* her emotional growth is expanded by her acceptance of the inadequacies of language as a communicative tool.

Laura's growth to adulthood is marked by a distinct shift in her
ability to understand words and their function. As a little girl in *Little House in the Big Woods,* she does not truly understand jokes, implied meanings, or double entendres, as illustrated in her missing the
point of Pa's parable about the man who cut two cat holes in his door
(*LHBW,* 22–23), or her not understanding why Pa calls her cousin
Charley a liar, "when he had not said a word" (*LHBW,* 211). To her,
a word has a meaning, and she does not expect, or even anticipate,
that the function of language exceeds that simplification.

In *Little House on the Prairie,* the book following *Little House in the
Big Woods,* Laura begins to be aware of the complexity of language,
particularly its inadequacy as a means of relaying one's innermost feelings. The event that triggers this discovery is especially emotionally
complex. When she watches the long line of Indians riding westward
past the house after the council of war, she longs to be with them.
First she claps her hands in excitement as the ponies parade past the
Ingalls cabin. Then her eyes catch those of a baby in a basket on its
mother's horse, and she begs her father to get it for her, not because
of any imperious desire on her part to own another human being, but

because the baby is, to her, a symbol of a part of herself that she does not know how to acknowledge. She has discovered an aspect of her own being that is inexpressible through language: it cannot be touched by the intellect, only by the heart.

To Laura, the baby represents a freedom to be part of the land-scape, an independence from the bonds of a society that demands sun-bonnets and neat braids. Laura tells her father that the Indian baby wants to be with her, although she actually means she wants to go with it. She begins to cry uncontrollably, and Ma asks in astonish-ment why Laura wants that baby. Laura's response is no answer to Ma's question, but it is the best she can do: " 'Its eyes are so black,' Laura sobbed. She could not say what she meant" (*LHP,* 309). She cannot explain why she is acting in this way because she does not un-derstand the profound reaction she is having. Words cannot express her deeply internalized motivation.

In the next book, *On the Banks on Plum Creek,* Laura realizes that language is not inflexible; it has "loopholes." She discovers that she can tell the truth and lie at the same time. Pa tells Laura and Mary not to slide down the straw-stack, and they promise not to. But, as Laura later points out to Mary, Pa has forbidden them only to slide down it; he has said nothing about climbing or rolling. When Pa finds the straw-stack demolished from their play, he asks them if they have disobeyed him by sliding down it. Both Laura and Mary tell him, quite truthfully, that they have not: " 'We did not slide, Pa,' Laura explained. 'But we did roll down it' " (*BPC,* 60). Laura has learned that language can be used to manipulate truth.

By the Shores of Silver Lake follows *On the Banks of Plum Creek,* and it is in this book that we can see the greatest change in Laura, for the entire family structure has been disrupted: Mary is blind. This forces additional maturation upon Laura. As Wilder wrote to her daughter, "Mary's blindness added to Laura's age."[4] Not only has Mary's sight gone, but with it has vanished her ability to communicate nonver-bally (*SSL,* 2). At this stage, Laura realizes, too, how much commu-nication is not reliant upon words but is expressed through the eyes.

Until Mary's sight is taken from her, Laura does not realize how much communication is nonverbal. Words are suddenly a vital source of communication and have a tremendous burden placed upon them. They must replace sight, and words are a poor substitute for any of the senses. Sensory deprivation cannot be equalized with language, but the task of making words compensate for the loss of sight is placed upon Laura, and her linguistic facility increases accordingly, for Mary rarely has to ask Laura to "see out loud" for her (*SSL*, 22–23).

The responsibility of being Mary's eyes brings with it frustration, for Mary has always been more literal than Laura. On their way to Silver Lake, Laura orally interprets the changing landscape for Mary, and Mary objects to Laura's description of the road as ending when it disappears behind a curve in the land. The road, Mary notes, continues to Silver Lake (*SSL*, 58).

Pa has the closest affinity to Laura in his way of seeing. When the family nears Silver Lake for the first time, Laura is aware that the land has somehow changed; it does not feel like the prairie they have known before. Pa voices the same feeling, and Ma points out, quite logically, that of course the land is different—their location has changed, and the vegetation has changed (*SSL*, 60). This is not, however, the difference that Laura and Pa perceive, yet neither can express precisely what they mean. Laura does not try, and Pa's efforts do not succeed. Part of the reason that Ma and Pa do not communicate well on this level is that Pa is using one sense, intuition, and Ma is using another, sight. They are not the same, nor do they share any commonality.

Mary's inability to cope with figurative language reappears a few pages later. Laura is describing to her two men riding into the sunset:

"Oh, Mary! The snow-white horse and the tall, brown man, with such a black head and a bright red shirt! The brown prairie all around—and they rode right into the sun as it was going down. They'll go on in the sun around the world."

Mary thought a moment. Then she said, "Laura, you know he couldn't ride into the sun. He's just riding along on the ground like anybody."

But Laura did not feel that she had told a lie. What she had said was true too. Somehow that moment when the beautiful, free pony and the wild man rode into the sun would last forever. (*SSL*, 65)

This passage is important in three ways: it shows Mary's difficulty in comprehending imagery; it reiterates the spiritual tug the West has on Laura (a restatement of the theme originally expressed in *Little House on the Prairie* when Laura begs Pa to get her the Indian baby); and it demonstrates how Wilder's colorful writing style developed first as an oral form.

The next incident of Laura's battle with the inefficiencies of language again involves Mary. In *The Long Winter,* Laura and Mary step outside between blizzards, and Mary objects to Laura's choice of the word "savage" to describe the bitterly cold air:

> "The air is only air," Mary replied. "You mean it is cold."
> "I don't either mean it's cold. I mean it's savage!" Laura snapped. (*LW,* 287)

Again Laura confronts the deficiencies of language. Weather is supposed to be incapable of expressing emotions such as hostility, yet to simply say that the air is "cold" is insufficient. It has a quality that is foreboding and dangerous; it is "savage."

Laura first experiences the power of words to overwhelm and control the emotional responses of others in *Little Town on the Prairie.* Reverend Brown, preaching a fire-and-brimstone sermon at a revival, asks the sinners in the congregation to come forward and repent. His voice overwhelms her, until she senses "something rising from all those people, something dark and frightening that grew and grew under that thrashing voice. The words no longer made sense, they were not sentences, they were only dreadful words" (*LTP,* 277). Until this point, Laura has been the one who controls words; now she understands that words can exercise a control of their own over people. But robbed of the cognitive base of language itself, words, she realizes, are nothing but sounds. A commonality of assumptions between speaker and audience must exist before communication can occur. It is precisely this commonality—or lack of it—that has prohibited her from being able to speak metaphorically with Mary: Mary, always the practical one, sees what is, not what could be, whereas Laura's eyes are constantly turned to the metaphorical West, to the future.

The next stage in the development of Laura's language skills occurs in *These Happy Golden Years.* It is at this stage in her life, in her midteens, that she begins to realize that even metaphor can have a literal truth. The catalyst for this discovery is Mr. Brewster, at whose house she is boarding while she teaches. He sits, Laura notes, "like a bump on a log." For the first time, she realizes how apropos the simile is: "A bump on a log does not fight anyone, but it cannot be budged" (*THGY,* 47). This new knowledge of the relationship between imagery and reality, of connotation's grounding in denotation—especially in metaphor—is another step in Laura's understanding the way language works.

The inadequacy of language that frustrates Laura reappears in a conversation she has with Ida Brown, the minister's daughter. While they stand on a hill looking westward at the Wessington Hills in the distance, Laura comments: "They are so beautiful they make me want to go to them." Ida responds that they are just ordinary hills. Again, Laura is frustrated by her inability to say what she means, because Ida's remark is, for Laura at any rate, only a partial truth; it does not touch the essential nature of the meaning the hills have for Laura: "In a way, that was true; and in another way, it wasn't. Laura could not say what she meant, but to her the Wessington Hills were more than grassy hills. Their shadowy outlines drew her with the lure of far places. They were the essence of a dream" (*THGY,* 153). As in the episodes with the Indian baby in *Little House on the Prairie* and the riders in the sunset in *By the Shores of Silver Lake,* Laura finds words incapable of expressing her thoughts. She has learned, however, that some things simply cannot be put into words, and she does not try to explain to Ida what she means, as she does in *Little House on the Prairie* when she becomes frustrated with her difficulty in explaining why she wants the baby. She has, at this point, accepted the insufficiency of words.

Laura does, however, know that words are not useless tools: they do have the power to bind one's future to certain acts, when used in promises. Just as she listened carefully to the words of the promise she made to her father in *On the Banks of Plum Creek,* so she approaches her marriage vows cautiously, telling Almanzo that she will not use the word *obey* in the service: "I can not make a promise that I will not keep, and, Almanzo, even if I tried, I do not think I could obey anybody against my better judgment" (*THGY,* 269–70). Almanzo recognizes the importance the word has for Laura, for on the way to the wedding, the only time he speaks is to confirm that Reverend Brown will not use the word *obey* in the ceremony.

In *The First Four Years,* words are one of the first indications Laura has of her pregnancy. As she watches the wheat being bagged, her eyes stray to the newspapers covering the walls of the shanty and she finds herself reading the words: "She was unreasonably annoyed because some of them were bottom side up but she must read them anyway. She couldn't take her eyes from them. Words! Words! The world was full of words and sliding wheat kernels!" (*FFY,* 45–46). The combination of words and wheat kernels represents the culmination of a lifetime of trying to reconcile factors that often seemed irreconcilable: the spiritual with the physical, the personal reaction with the public expression.

Through her growth and perception of the prairie world, she has come to know herself and her position in relation to the world. Much of Laura's growth to adulthood is dependent upon her realization of a wider world than she has initially perceived as her preconceptions are challenged. Her world is no longer marked by words such as "safe," "snug," or "cosy," because she realizes that the world is not any of those, nor would she want it to be, and that those adjectives gain meaning only through knowledge of their opposites, that "safe" has value only if one has known "un-safe," "snug" if one has known "un-snug," "cosy" if one has known "un-cosy." The boundaries she has ascribed to the world are expanded, while those of language, she discovers, are much more limited. It is through the acceptance of these new boundaries and their integration into her own life that she understands the eternal struggle—of Laura and language, of pioneer and prairie, of individual and the world.

Chapter Six

Farmer Boy: Almanzo's Story

Farmer Boy, Wilder's second novel, is the only book she wrote that does not contain Laura as the main character. It is, instead, Almanzo Wilder's story. This alone makes it unique in the body of Wilder's work, and therefore meriting an independent study, but it must also be compared to the other *Little House* books, for the change of protagonists is only one of the differences between this book and the others.

At first glance, *Farmer Boy* seems to have no plot; it is simply the story of a young boy's wish to grow up. There is little tension in such a story line, for even the most naive reader recognizes that there is no other possible resolution than that the boy's wish be realized—nature will take care of that. Underlying this simplistic plot, however, is a theme so subtle that it is a graceful accomplishment in the field of often didactic children's literature. It is the interpretation of "big enough," a phrase that appears repeatedly throughout the novel, which begins shortly before Almanzo's ninth birthday.

More than anything else, Almanzo wants a horse. But he must wait for his father's approval, and that depends upon his father's being convinced that Almanzo can bear the responsibility of owning and caring for a horse, a state Almanzo calls "big enough." The youngest in the Wilder family, Almanzo doubts at times that he will ever grow up, for he is teetering on the edge of little-boyhood, no longer a baby and not yet an adult. When he brags to his cousin Frank that he is going to have his own colt, and Frank jeers at him, Almanzo becomes discouraged, questioning "if he would ever be big enough to have anything he wanted" (*FB,* 92). He is too big to sit in the front of the wagon and hold the ends of the reins, pretending to drive while his father does the actual work, but he is too young to drive the horses himself. This situation of being neither one nor the other both frustrates and depresses him.

The fact that he is smaller than his brother Royal and his father underscores his problem, for he cannot help but compare himself against them, and he often pales in the contrast. Even his shoes are different; he must wear mocassins instead of boots since his feet are still growing (*FB*, 30–31). When his father surprises him by having the cobbler make him boots instead of replacing his worn-out mocassins with new ones, Almanzo is pleased, especially when his father answers Almanzo's mother's objection with, "He's big enough now to wear boots" (*FB*, 289).

Yet Almanzo does sense that there is more to maturity than its physical aspects, and he tries very hard to demonstrate his capabilities. Often he is impatient with the languid pace his journey to adulthood seems to be taking, and he attempts to speed it up. When he tries to prove himself to his father, he sometimes makes mistakes. Caused by an overzealousness to show his competency, Almanzo's errors are nevertheless a natural part of learning.

In trying to hurry the natural process along, he places pressure on himself to stop being a little boy, and he agonizes over his mistakes, chastising himself for his quite natural childish impulsiveness. While watching the men chop ice, in his excitement and involvement with the activity he forgets to be cautious and runs for a closer look at the work. At the edge of the hole the men have cut, he stumbles. French Joe, one of the hired men, catches him by the leg just before he slides headlong into the freezing water. Almanzo scolds himself for his recklessness: "A boy nine years old is too big to do foolish things because he doesn't stop to think. Almanzo knew that, and felt ashamed" (*FB*, 70).

At the Fourth of July celebration, he struggles with the conflicting desires of being a little boy and being a man. He is challenged again by Frank, who has a nickel, to prove that his father would give him one, too, if he asked. Almanzo's feet lag as he approaches his father to ask for the money, because he is terrified: afraid to ask such a favor of his father and frightened that his father will refuse to give him the nickel and thus embarrass him in front of his cousin. He knows he should not ask, but perched between boyhood and young adulthood, he does anyway, forced into doing so by his cousin's "double dare" (*FB*, 181), the childhood test of courage. By allowing himself and his actions to be influenced by others, his peer group, he shows that his maturity is not complete; yet by sensing that asking such a favor for such a reason is wrong, he shows an evolving sense of responsibility. Furthermore, by investing the half-dollar that his father gives him in a piglet instead of lemonade, he shows his ability to think ahead, one of the indications of maturity.

In the chapter entitled "Wood-Hauling," Almanzo refuses to make concessions to his size and that of his sled and oxen, which are year-lings like himself. His father's sled is already loaded, and when Al-manzo adds the last log to his own smaller sled, the log falls on him. His father tells him to be more careful in the future, for "men must look out for themselves in the timber" (*FB*, 335). Almanzo hurts so much that he apparently does not realize that his father has included him in the very group to which he is seeking admittance—men.

Almanzo's next mistake is trying to copy the large loads the men are hauling. Unfortunately he overloads his sled and has difficulty in getting the sled—or the yearlings—to move. His father explains to him that if he does not adjust the load to fit the road conditions, he could ruin the oxen (*FB*, 337). That he might spoil something as hardy as a team of oxen does not bode well for a little boy who wants to be entrusted with a delicate animal like a colt.

Almanzo's developing sense of responsibility is shown in his atti-tude toward those things under his care, most notably the piglet and a pumpkin. Yet they are both, in a way, a source of frustration to him. He can see them growing, getting noticeably bigger as the sum-mer wears on. Unfortunately, he does not see that he, too, is grow-ing; at least the pace is not what he would like. So he tries the same tactic on himself that he uses on the piglet and the pumpkin: he tries to eat more food. Just as he "force-feeds" milk to the pumpkin through a length of candlewicking and gives the piglet all the food she can eat, he makes himself drink more milk and eat more food. Although his father mildly chastises him at dinner for not eating ev-erything Almanzo piles on his plate, the boy continues to force him-self to eat more, because he believes that will help him "grow up faster so he could help break the colts" (*FB*, 192).

Almanzo's pumpkin is larger than any of the others displayed at the fair, but his father warns him that size alone will not win him the prize: "It isn't size that counts as much as quality" (*FB*, 267). Almanzo's father could easily be speaking about a little boy as well as about a pumpkin.

When his pumpkin wins the blue ribbon and he is asked how he grew it, he is caught by qualms of uncertainty. He wonders if he has perhaps broken the rules by entering a milk-fed pumpkin, and con-siders the consequences of telling the judge how he raised the pump-kin. If he has broken a rule, he might lose the ribbon and be labeled a cheat. He is in a quandary about how to answer the judge's question. His decision seems to be governed by his father's presence: he does not want his father to hear him tell a lie. Only afterward does he realize that his father would not have let him enter a milk-fed pumpkin if doing so violated the rules of the competition; his father would never let him do something that was wrong. This belated comprehension shows that Almanzo's analytical process is not quite matured.

What Almanzo fails to realize is that maturity, although an undeniable physical adjunct to chronological age, cannot be measured in terms of years. It is measured by one's ability to analyze problems, make sensible decisions, and assume responsibility. And a determination of an individual's maturity must be based on cumulative evidence.

Within *Farmer Boy,* a momentum of incidents exists, carefully structured to show a maturity that is developing slowly but developing nevertheless. A major indication of maturity is the ability to learn from the past. When Almanzo receives two hundred dollars for returning a lost wallet to its owner, he decides to put the money in the bank rather than spend it right away, figuring that he can buy his own colt with it (*FB,* 360–61). Although he is not aware of it, he has taken to heart the lesson his father taught him on Independence Day: that he can do what he wants with his money, but some choices will prove wiser than others.

Mixed in with his own awareness of himself are ways others see him. In the last chapter, Almanzo takes steps to decide his own future, perhaps the ultimate mark of maturity. Mr. Paddock has offered to apprentice Almanzo at the wagon-shop, and Almanzo's parents discuss the proposal. When his father says that they will have to let him go if he wants to, his mother objects to having the decision passed on to their son, claiming, "He's too young to know his own mind" (*FB,* 369). But his father, to whom Almanzo had directed his efforts at appearing adult, asks the boy what his opinion is, and thus shows that he has begun to respect his son's judgment, even about such an important choice—the mark of recognized maturity.

Almanzo is surprised that his father is letting him determine the course of his life; he has assumed he would have to do his father's bidding. When Almanzo's father encourages him to think about whether he would rather live in town or on a farm, Almanzo realizes he already knows what he wants; he wants to be just like his father, yet he is reluctant to say so directly. Almanzo's response is more symbolic than straightforward: "I want a colt" (*FB*, 371), and by his ability to answer metaphorically, he displays a developed sense of maturity.

Published a year after *Little House in the Big Woods, Farmer Boy* follows its predecessor in style, although not in story. The immediate similarity is the basic approach. *Farmer Boy* is written in the same semibiographical style as the *Little House* books. The main character, Almanzo Wilder, is based upon Wilder's husband, as Laura Ingalls is based upon Laura Ingalls Wilder as a young girl.

The opening passage of *Farmer Boy* is reminiscent of that of *Little House in the Big Woods. Farmer Boy* begins: "It was January in northern New York State, sixty-seven years ago" (*FB*, 1). The description of the snow-covered landscape in the first paragraph establishes the mood and draws a strong visual image. The field of vision then narrows quickly—from New York State to one road to the people on that road, beginning with "a little boy trudged to school" (*FB*, 1). This rapid downshift, which creates a feeling of isolation, centers immediately on the characters, focusing on the one who will be the main character.

Little House in the Big Woods begins: "Once upon a time, sixty years ago, a little girl lived in the Big Woods of Wisconsin" (*LHBW*, 1). This immediate focusing of time and place and the introduction of the main character as a generic figure ("a little boy" and "a little girl") illustrate the structural similarities between the two works. Both novels span approximately a year, which allows Wilder to develop the detail that marks her writing.

Occasionally a line occurs in *Farmer Boy* that harks back to *Little House in the Big Woods:* "So everything was snug and comfortable in the house" (*FB*, 62) picks up the theme and even the language of "They were cosy and comfortable in their little house made of logs" (*LHBW*, 44), providing a continuity between the books.

The repetition of key phrases and themes that contributes to the mood in *Little House in the Big Woods* does not, however, work so well in *Farmer Boy,* perhaps because the repetitions contain negative emotions rather than the positive "cosy" ones of *Little House in the Big Woods*. The emphasis on Almanzo's not being "big enough" to have his own colt sometimes results in nearly direct duplications: "When Almanzo thought that it would be years and years before he could hold the reins and drive horses like that, he could hardly bear it" (*FB*, 89) and "When he thought that it would be years and years before he could have a little colt to teach and take care of, he could hardly bear it" (*FB*, 142). Such reinforcement seems awkward and, in fact, unnecessary in a story clearly about a boy who wants to grow up enough to have his own colt.

Despite the similarities between the novels, *Farmer Boy* is, in several ways, quite different from the other *Little House* books. The human struggle with the land that is a recurring theme in the other *Little House* books is not present in *Farmer Boy*, nor is any contrast drawn between the ferocious and the extraordinarily beautiful character of the land. There is no inherent threat to add tension to the story line. The sole conflict is one that has only one resolution: Almanzo will grow up.

Laura Ingalls Wilder does not seem comfortable with the area or the bounty of her husband's childhood farm: she was not familiar with either and had to rely on his recollections. Because the farm is an established and successful operation, she is often forced to deal with the made rather than with the making. Wilder is at her best describing nature, and never seems quite at ease with buildings. The description of the barns (*FB*, 14–15) seems to lack vitality, although the descriptions of Almanzo's mother weaving (*FB*, 61) and the cobbler making shoes (*FB*, 292–95), because they both involve activity and the creation of something, are interesting.

Farmer Boy seems to lack the guiding focus of the *Little House* books. This may be due to the fact that the *Little House* books are expanded versions of the "Pioneer Girl" manuscript, which deals only with Laura. Wilder quickly conceived the concept of using the manuscript as the basis of a multivolume historical novel. It is doubtful, however, that at the time she wrote *Farmer Boy* she envisioned it as an introduction to a character who would play an important role in Laura's later life. It may be that *Farmer Boy* was written with the idea that it, too, could be developed into an independent series, yet the evidence for this assertion is insufficient. In addition, the *Little House* books are not so much the story of Laura, but the story of the settlement of the frontier. What a series developed from *Farmer Boy* would have utilized as its overall theme is unclear.

Nevertheless, as the shape of the multivolume historical novel took form, *Farmer Boy* assumed its place in the series by establishing Almanzo as a major figure. It laid the foundation of Almanzo's character, prepared the psychology for the ensuing relationship between Laura and Almanzo, and added a dimension to the frontier story by bringing in a major character whose childhood roots were in the East and yet who did not cling to the memories of the East as the ultimate standard, the basis of comparison for life on the prairie.

Almanzo also adds a dimension to the frontier experience chronicled by the *Little House* books in that he represents the young pioneer who is determined yet kind and cheerful. In some ways he is like Laura's father, or the way Pa would have been had he not been weighted with family cares. The characteristics Almanzo displays as an adult are shown in their developmental stage in *Farmer Boy,* and it is thus that the story of Almanzo's childhood gains a position in the *Little House* saga.

One would expect such a character to identify strongly with the land. Almanzo shows no such tendency. He seems, in fact, usually to be unaware of his surroundings. Even when he is, Wilder is faced with the stylistic problem of how to describe that awareness. She cannot allow him to become a male Laura; he must retain his own identity and personality.

Almanzo seems strangely detached at times, a sharp contrast to the intensely alert Laura, who is always listening, watching, absorbing. The reader knows how she feels, which is frequently not the way good little girls are "supposed" to feel. She is spirited, and can be angry, naughty, envious—all very real emotions, thus making her character multifaceted or multidimensional and always interesting. The very fact that she is interested makes her interesting. Almanzo's flashes of emotion are few. His sister Alice is perhaps closer to Laura in personality. For instance, after the children have eaten most of the sugar while their parents are gone, Alice says, "There's *some* sugar left. Mother said, 'Don't eat *all* the sugar,' and we didn't. There's some around the edges" (*FB,* 219), a fine distinction that Laura picks up in the later *On the Banks of Plum Creek* when she and Mary destroy a haystack by climbing and rolling on it, but not by sliding down it, as they had been forbidden to do.

The point of view Wilder employs in *Farmer Boy* contributes to the sense of detachment. Rather than limiting herself to Almanzo's point of view, she sometimes adopts the stance of the omniscient narrator. When she describes his cold cheeks as "red as apples" and his nose "redder than a cherry" (*FB,* 4), she is using the observation of a third party: Almanzo cannot possibly see his own cheeks, although he may be able to see a portion of his nose. Later Wilder's daughter Rose lectured her about the relationship between this sort of description and point of view, noting that describing effect rather than appearance was more expressive.

This omniscient point of view creates an incongruity in the last chapter of the book. When Mother and Father discuss Mr. Paddock's offer to apprentice Almanzo at the wagon-shop, he listens but he does not seem mentally involved with the conversation, although it concerns him and his future. He should be fiercely interested, for if he goes to work for Mr. Paddock, his entire life will be changed. Just as the conversation begins to gather momentum, it is interrupted by a two-paragraph description of what he is eating (*FB*, 368–69). This would seem to imply that his attention is diverted from the conversation to his food, a strange turn of events when his future is at stake. One would expect him to stop eating and listen intently. For food to take precedence at this particular moment is odd, especially since it would indicate that he cannot concentrate on important things—and it is, in essence, a conversation about maturity.

Almanzo appears as a character in the later books of the *Little House* saga, and Wilder used *Farmer Boy* as a basis for the affinity of spirit that would later link her two main characters, Laura and Almanzo.

Farmer Boy displays elements that are repeated in other *Little House* books. The sense of responsibility, which Almanzo learns in *Farmer Boy,* becomes an integral facet of his personality in *The Long Winter* where he exhibits a keen feeling of community responsibility and carries out perhaps the ultimate in responsible action. The phrase "free and independent" is repeated from *Farmer Boy* as the title of the chapter in *The Long Winter* in which Almanzo decides to go after wheat for the townspeople, although he has seed wheat himself. He knows he can make a profit by selling his seed wheat, as his brother Royal recommends, but he recognizes that by doing so he will lose his chance to be "free and independent." Once he has decided not to sell his seed wheat, he then must decide what to do about the community's needs, for the people are starving. Perhaps to absolve himself from the decision not to sell his wheat (he could sell it and thus provide at least a temporary solution to the community's problem), he decides that he will undertake the perilous journey to get the wheat from another settler outside of town.

The chapter entitled "Independence Day" is echoed in *Little Town on the Prairie*'s "Fourth of July," and the same elements are present: the lemonade, the reading of the Declaration of Independence, the feeling of solemnity the protagonists experience during the ceremony.

In addition, the horses that are so important in *Farmer Boy* are picked up and utilized again. As Almanzo races his team of Morgans in the buggy race, Laura silently cheers for him, her attention seemingly focused on his horses, as it was the first time she saw him from a distance at the end of *By the Shores of Silver Lake* and at a closer proximity at the beginning of *The Long Winter*. But this concentration on the horses is, in a unique way, shown to be self-deception on Laura's part, for the other characters seem to evaporate. The limiting of the characters and the focusing of attention on Laura and Almanzo and the horses introduce the delicately restrained attraction.

The setting of *Farmer Boy* adds balance to the series as a whole by providing the backdrop of "the East" that prairie conditions will be juxtaposed against. The contrast of comfort and ease with the harsh reality of the prairie contributes an extra dimension to prairie life. In developing a sense of what the United States was like as a nation at the time, the reader of the *Little House* books is tacitly asked to consider why anyone would leave this comfort and is challenged to discover why the settling of the West occurred at all. Perhaps in the *Little House* books, through the visions of both Laura and Almanzo, the question is answered.

Chapter Seven

"So Many Ways of Seeing Things and So Many Ways of Saying Them"

The *Little House* books have been praised for several reasons: they are historically accurate, they are true to the innate nature of a child, and they portray an American family's interworkings in an odyssey through childhood. Above all, it is the way in which they are written that has guaranteed the books' place among the classics of American literature.

Wilder's natural talent for writing was developed under the tutorial guidance of her daughter, Rose Wilder Lane, an accomplished novelist and journalist herself. She steered her mother's literary ventures, sometimes with the light touch of suggestion, sometimes with the heavier hand of lecture.

Lane played an active role in her mother's career. She was responsible for marketing Wilder's books to an agent, but perhaps more importantly she served as teacher and editor. The correspondence between her and her mother could, in fact, serve as an excellent text in creative writing. Lane firmly believed that writing skills could be taught. As she wrote her mother in 1924, after the sale of one of her mother's articles: "You didn't really believe me. ********** it all, you've just GOT to believe me, now."[1]

Lane's encouragement and assurances to her often doubting mother clarify which talents Wilder possessed innately and which were developed. Lane pointed out that Wilder's descriptions, particularly of landscapes, were "perfect." A recurring problem, though, was structure and, to a lesser degree, point of view. Their correspondence is replete with reminders and advice about structure and point of view. Even with Lane's editorial corrections, Wilder's first book had to undergo some changes at Harper and Brothers; Virginia Kirkus, the editor of the children's book department, wrote her: "In some instances you have had the stories told by a person in the main story, and put into the first person, in other instances it has been thrown into the third person. This results in some confusion and shifts the emphasis inaccurately."[2]

The extent of Lane's work on the Wilder manuscripts can best be illustrated by examining *The First Four Years,* which Lane apparently did not edit.[3] The manuscript of the book, entitled "The First Three Years and a Year of Grace," was discovered after Wilder's death. Because the events in the book follow those treated in the last *Little House* volume published during Wilder's lifetime, *These Happy Golden Years* (1943), the natural assumption was made that the book was written after *These Happy Golden Years.* In his 1970 introduction to *The First Four Years,* Roger Lea MacBride posited his belief that Wilder began writing the book in the latter part of the 1940s and subsequently abandoned the project due to her despondency over her husband's death in 1949 (*FFY,* xiv).

As plausible as that hypothesis was, certain inconsistencies perplexed Wilder scholars. The book was markedly different from the other *Little House* books. It lacked the sparkle that had highlighted the preceding volumes; a "flatly told"[4] narrative with little dialogue or extended description, it seemed more of a factual accounting of the early years of Wilder's marriage than part of the *Little House* novel. Laura's previous optimism and spirited zest is diminished, and although the misfortunes that plagued the newlyweds would indeed cause despair in anyone, the negativism that pervades the book begins before the first disheartening episode as Laura uncharacteristically expresses her reservations about marrying a farmer and hints about living in town (*FFY,* 3–6), a curiously different reaction from the one Laura of *These Happy Golden Years* has when Almanzo asks if she minds that they will be starting out poor: "I have always lived in little houses. I like them" (*THGY,* 215).

Material from *These Happy Golden Years* reappears in *The First Four Years.* That such repetition was intentional is dubious for, as Rosa Ann Moore observed, it occurs in none of Wilder's other works.[5] The prologue in *The First Four Years* seems to duplicate chapters 22 and 23 in *These Happy Golden Years* as Laura sings "In the Starlight" while she and Almanzo are out riding in the evening, although in *The First Four Years* the scene occurs in June, and in *These Happy Golden Years* it is late August or early September. In addition, the last three chapters of *These Happy Golden Years* are retold in *The First Four Years.*

Moore was among the first to suspect that the date Wilder was believed to have written *The First Four Years* was incorrect,[6] but it was not until William T. Anderson examined the manuscript of *The First Four Years* ("The First Three Years and a Year of Grace") that any conclusive evidence was brought to the theory that *The First Four Years* had probably been written earlier than had been believed.

Anderson based his theory in part on his knowledge of Wilder's work habits. In the initial stages of her writing career, Wilder composed her works on cheap tablets, writing in pencil on both sides of the sheets. "The First Three Years and a Year of Grace" is written in this fashion. She also economically used the reverse sides of letters and other scratch paper for rough drafts. By examining the paper upon which the manuscript was written, Anderson discovered a probable date for the composition of "The First Three Years and a Year of Grace." One was a letter dated 20 January 1933, and the other was a manuscript page from *Farmer Boy*, written in 1932.[7] It was unlikely that even the thrifty Wilder would have kept scratch paper for fifteen years.

Anderson also noted that the way the manuscript was divided into a prologue and four chapters seemed closer to the style in which "Pioneer Girl," Wilder's first lengthy literary attempt (1930), had been constructed with no chapter divisions,[8] a marked contrast with the thirty-three chapters of *These Happy Golden Years*. In addition, he observed that the manuscript bears evidence of Wilder's early uncertainty about phrasing and composition; the numerous deletions and additions in Wilder's hand found in "The First Three Years and a Year of Grace" mark the manuscripts of only her early works.[9]

Although it is impossible to ascertain the precise date of the composition of "The First Three Years and a Year of Grace," the testimony of the manuscript itself suggests an approximate composition date near 1933. Such a date would resolve the paradoxes *The First Four Years* has presented scholars. Because it is unedited by her daughter, *The First Four Years* allows scholars to examine which aspects of Wilder's writing formed the basis of her craft; description, as Lane told her, was her forte, and the descriptive passages from *The First Four Years* support Lane's assessment. An analysis of the development of Wilder's adeptness with the other components of writing, and an investigation into the role they played in the overall effectiveness of her style reveal much about her technique. It is useful not only to trace the evolution of Wilder's craft, but to examine which aspects received the most emphasis both from the author and from her daughter-editor.

The style of the *Little House* books succeeds on many levels. The unusual way in which the books were conceptualized as a series with the level of reading increasing with each succeeding volume contributes to its stature in the ranks of serial novels. The unique point of view Wilder adopts in the *Little House* books, that of a main character who bears the same name as the author, lends an air of credence to the plot. The theme, the plot, the tone, and the enthusiastic American pride found in the books have had great appeal not only in the United States but abroad, as evidenced by their translation into several languages. Imagery and personification bring life to Wilder's narrative, and complement the precise characterization that allows children to recognize aspects of themselves in a little girl who lived one hundred years ago.

Yet describing aspects of Wilder's prose style is not sufficient for revealing her technique. One must look not so much at what she did but at how and why she did it to understand her craft, and that can be accomplished by analyzing her prose in terms of its component parts: point of view, theme, plot, tone, imagery, personification, and characterization.

Point of View

Wilder maintains an unusual point of view throughout the *Little House* series. She is the main character and clearly identifies herself as such by specifically naming her main character "Laura Ingalls" and using her full name, "Laura Ingalls Wilder," as author. Thus, even before the entrance of Almanzo Wilder at the end of *By the Shores of Silver Lake,* the reader senses an additional touch of realism in the writing; he or she knows that the story's "Laura" is the author and that the book is more than an absolute fiction. This point of view lends an air of authenticity to the story.

In her early attempts at writing the story of her life, Wilder struggled with which voice to adopt. In the "Pioneer Girl" manuscript, she used the first person, and in "When Grandma Was a Little Girl" she began with "Grandma" and then switched to "Laura" in the fifth paragraph. This approach was abandoned in favor of the consistent "Laura." Wilder's correspondence with her daughter suggests that Wilder apparently found it easier to write in the first person.[10]

Because the experiences of childhood in the late nineteenth century may be alien to the twentieth-century child, point of view becomes very important as a means of adding credibility to the material. Wilder must show her audience that while Laura's experiences are unique to her time, Laura is not. She must have the feelings and reactions of a child in any time, in any environment.

Writing from the limited omniscient point of view rather than the first-person (biographical or autobiographical) point of view allows Wilder to explore beyond Laura's acknowledged perceptions. The reader knows that Laura sees the flowers on the prairie, for instance, without the flowers being a conscious intrusion in the narrative, as they would have been had Laura written the books in the first person. In one of her letters to her mother about the art of writing, Rose Wilder Lane lectured Wilder extensively about point of view: "You MUST keep in mind to write the whole thing from Laura's point of view. Arrange the material so that she can actually see, hear, experience as much as possible. And remember that 'Laura' means 'I,' and that the past tense is present."[11]

This point of view enables Laura to grow up in the series while retaining the observation and voice suitable to the experience appropriate to Laura's age in any given book. Had Wilder chosen the first-person point of view, Laura would have been forced into commenting on her own maturity as she saw it; instead, the reader senses her growing up—her maturation is reflected in her attitudes, in the attitudes of those who surround her, and in her speech and behavior.

Wilder violates her own strict sense of point of view in two of her books: *Farmer Boy* and *The Long Winter*. In *The Long Winter* she relates several events that occur outside Laura's field of vision. Perhaps the retention of a restricted point of view in such a book, in which Laura rarely is able even to step outside the house in town because the weather is severe, would not allow a break in the overwhelming "sameness" of the setting, although Laura herself is never allowed such a break. Limiting the material to Laura's perceptions would have meant limiting the scope of the book to the confines of the house, and often to one room.

It is important to note, however, that such shifts in the point of view are complete in themselves. In *The Long Winter,* Wilder attempts to identify her introductions of "new" voices by placing such passages at the beginnings or ends of chapters or by isolating them in separate chapters. Wilder is obviously not comfortable with total omniscience, or even with an expanded limited omniscience. In the chapter entitled "Antelope," during which Pa and some of the men from the town go hunting for antelope, Wilder switches back and forth between calling Pa "Pa" and "Mr. Ingalls." In this chapter, the point of view shifts more frequently than in any other. It begins with Laura's, changes to a shared one (Pa and Almanzo's), returns to Laura's, and then changes to Pa's. Such rapid shifts make the chapter seem awkward, perhaps because Wilder was trying to introduce Almanzo as an important character at the same time as she was trying to relate a crucial incident. These events occur outside the house-bound Laura's point of view; the only other way Wilder could have managed to include this information would have been to revert to the "story within a story" structure used in *Little House in the Big Woods*. Despite Lane's advice to "STAY INSIDE LAURA!"[12] certain demands of the plot required Wilder to expand the point of view.

Had Wilder written the *Little House* books in the first person, they would have been undeniably autobiography, and had she chosen a consistent third-person omniscient viewpoint, they would have been clearly fiction. By choosing to address her subject from a limited third-person point of view, Wilder effectively retains the "real" identity of Laura while avoiding the strictures required by autobiography.

Theme, Plot, and Tone

In Wilder's work, theme, plot, and tone intertwine into an inseparable whole. Wilder's daughter Rose advised Wilder to determine the theme of each book before proceeding further with the writing. While they were struggling with the opening of *By the Shores of Silver Lake,* Lane wrote her mother:

> It seems to me that this book is about railroad- and town-building. Is it?
> These themes are mixed up with homesteading, and with the lonely winter in the surveyors' house. PLUM CREEK didn't fall into a coherent pattern until after a lot of fumbling and waste time and work you wrote me that its theme was the wheat crop. Let's get the theme of this one clear right away.[13]

The theme, Lane pointed out, determined at what point in time the book should start, but Wilder felt that the tone was equally important. She wanted *By the Shores of Silver Lake* to begin at the depot, but Lane believed that beginning the action at the house at Plum

Creek, with Aunt Docia's arrival, was more in keeping with the theme of railroad and town. In a letter to Lane, Wilder clarified that the theme was not building, but homesteading, and questioned what effect starting the book at the Plum Creek house would have on the reader, noting, "It would begin the story with a recital of discouragements and calamities such as Mary's sickness & blindness. I *don't like it!*"[14] A few days later she added that she was concerned with the tone such a beginning would set: "The readers must know all that [about Mary's blindness and the family's setbacks] but they should not be made to think about it."[15] She found Lane's opening too depressing and asked, "But how to write that chapter and not have it too sad."[16]

Wilder conceded to her daughter's wishes about the opening of *By the Shores of Silver Lake*. The first chapter is structured as Lane desired, and the theme is firmly established as Pa's excitement about the prospect of homesteading and Ma's reluctance to leave her settled home dominate the chapter. Their emotions stand out like sparks against the flat narrative of the financial straits and desperate situation the Ingalls family faces at Plum Creek. The second chapter introduces the audience to an adolescent Laura, now almost thirteen years old. It is a necessary chapter, for almost five years have elapsed since the end of the preceding book, *On the Banks of Plum Creek*. The third chapter quickly moves the location of the story to the train depot, and the story of homesteading begins. Thus, both Wilder and her daughter are satisfied. The first two chapters are merely introductory chapters, and the story does not actually begin until the third.

The Long Winter requires a plot structure different from those of the other books in the series. Correlating the plot and the theme of this book created a problem for Wilder. In a letter to her daughter, she discussed the difficulty she was having with the structure:

Here is what is bothering me and holding me up. I can't seem to find a plot, or pattern as you call it.
There seems to be nothing to it only the struggle to live, through the winter, until spring comes again. . . . But is it strong enough, or can it be made strong enough to supply the necessary thread running all through the book. I could make the book with the plot being Laura's struggles to be, and success in becoming a teacher. With the Hard Winter and all being obstacles overcome on the way. . . . That would be a plot. . . . But it seems to weaken it. . . . But where is the plot in Hard Winter?[17]

The theme of *The Long Winter,* the battle between the weather and the settlers, demands a clear resolution, one in which either the elements or the people win. The structure Wilder eventually used is that of the conventional novel, with rising and falling action based around one major climactic point. The conflict mounts as the relentless onslaught of blizzards erodes the settlers' physical and emotional resources. The appearance of the gentle chinook wind, a sharp contrast to the harsh blizzard winds, seems to announce the denouement. But it is a false resolution. The town still faces starvation, for all that is left to eat is a rapidly dwindling store of wheat. Another month passes before the conflict is finally resolved with the arrival of a freight train carrying supplies.

The structure of the *Little House* books becomes involved if one views the series as Wilder envisioned it, as a multivolume historical novel[18] or as one continuing story. If the volumes are viewed as a whole, certain repetitions occur. For instance, in the series Pa builds a floor three times. That the author condenses the episode further each time it appears shows Wilder's recognition of narrative structure. In *Little House on the Prairie,* Wilder describes Pa's making a puncheon floor in great detail, over the span of three pages (*LHP,* 127–29). The next time Pa builds a floor, the description is compacted into two lines (*BPC,* 111). And the last time Pa builds a floor, it occurs outside the narrative action of the story entirely (*SSL,* 264).

Recurring motifs in the scenes with Indians add symbolic significance to the theme of the *Little House* books and clarify Laura's character by showing how adulthood wrought changes in her priorities. In *Little House on the Prairie* the episode in which Laura's eyes catch and hold those of an Indian baby as the Osage leave Lesser Reserve is one of the most emotion-laden incidents of the series (*LHP,* 307–11). It shows her early identification with the native people of the prairie, while it also reveals her confusion about her own identity. She wants to be one of them, yet she also wants the baby to stay with her in the little house. She wants to go, to be a part of another life-style, yet she does not want to abandon her own. She would like to be able to incorporate the two life-styles—that of the Native Americans, which represents a certain kind of freedom, with her own, which provides her with security through its restrictions. At the same time, she is experiencing the distressing realization that the "now is now" (*LHBW,* 238) philosophy she accepted so readily only a short while before as an aspect of her security can also be painful as a moment passes by, untouchable and unreclaimable. Her responses to all of what is occurring, not just in front of her, but inside her, are so complex that they are beyond her understanding, and she cannot stop crying.

Later, in *The First Four Years,* five Indians come to the Wilder house and Laura sees them go into the barn where her pony Trixie is. Because she is angry, she forgets her adult inclination to be cautious and runs out to the barn. She slaps one of the Indians when he touches her arm.

It made him angry and he started toward her, but the other Indians laughed, and one who seemed to be the leader stopped him. Then with signs pointing to himself, his pony, and then with a sweep of his arm toward the west, he said, "You go—me—be my squaw?"

Laura shook her head, and stamping her foot again, motioned them all to their ponies and away, telling them to go.

And they went, riding their running ponies without saddles or bridles.

But as they went their leader turned and looked back at Laura where she stood, with the wind blowing her skirts around her and her braids flying, watching them go away across the prairie into the west. (*FFY,* 33–35)

In *The First Four Years,* the participants in the *Little House on the Prairie* scene have grown up, and their reactions are different—they are acting as adults, not as children. Laura finally has the chance to fulfill her childhood desire, to go with the Indian baby on horses that "did not have to wear bridles or saddles" (*LHP,* 307) and to ride into the west, but she refuses. Her eyes lock with the Indian leader's as they did with the Indian baby's years ago, while the Indians move on and leave her behind. This time, however, it is by her choice. It is her final rejection of childhood.

The repetition of elements throughout the series contributes to the overall tone—one of optimism in the face of adversity—and to the theme of the steadfastness of the family and the self. Such recurrences also accentuate the continuity of the story, so that it can be viewed as one complete novel rather than nine discrete books.

Imagery and Personification

The use of imagery heightens the immediacy of the narrative moment through the appeal to the reader's senses. Wilder uses imagery in the *Little House* books to recreate her protagonists' experiences as completely as possible and to act as interpretive commentary on those experiences.

The most commonly used sense is vision. Details of everyday occurrences are noted, thus helping to recreate Laura's or Almanzo's environment as they perceive it and to share with the twentieth-century reader experiences that are not a part of his or her life.

Laura watches carefully, and her observations are filled with the detail of daily life on the American frontier. The detail is so specific that the reader feels as if he or she knows how to build a door or smoke-cure pork after reading a passage showing one of the Ingalls family in such a pursuit. Wilder avoids letting the material become sheerly informational by the inclusion of Wilder's sensory reactions, which move such factual passages into the mainstream of the story.

Wilder uses vision, and color in particular, to focus the narrative. Usually her color "portraits" concentrate on the prairie and reflect Wilder's satisfaction with her surroundings. This is especially apparent in *Little House on the Prairie* once Laura has accepted the prairie. She then is capable of seeing and appreciating the beauty of the land, which had originally seemed so austere. As Laura begins to explore her new environment, she notices the variety of colors it contains and discovers how much it has to offer her observant and curious eye.

Wilder frequently describes the "glory of colors" (*LTP*, 4) of the sunrises: "The sky was very faintly pink, then it was pinker. The colour went higher up the sky. It grew brighter and deeper. It blazed like fire, and suddenly the little cloud was glittering gold. In the centre of the blazing colour, on the flat edge of the earth, a tiny sliver of sun appeared. It was a short streak of white fire. Suddenly the whole sun bounded up, round and huge, far bigger than the ordinary sun and throbbing with so much light that its roundness almost burst" (*BPC*, 46).[19] She also creates tonal pictures of sunsets on the prairie. The diction of the sunset descriptions is different from that of the sunrise descriptions, however. The sunrises are described with an exuberance that is replaced by majesty in the sunsets: "The sun was sinking to rest, like a king, Laura thought, drawing the gorgeous curtains of his great bed around him. . . . 'The sun is sinking, Mary, into white downy clouds that spread to the edge of the world. All the tops of them are crimson, and streaming down from the top of the sky are great gorgeous curtains of rose and gold with pearly edges. They are a great canopy over the whole prairie. The little streaks of sky between them are clear, pure green' " (*LTP*, 110–11).

The language of the sunset descriptions is drawn out by the long vowel sounds: the assonance of the long *e* in "streaming," "streaks," and "green" in the passage from *Little Town on the Prairie* forces the movement of the language to slow. The language of the sunrise descriptions, however, depends upon the explosive consonant sounds: the repetition of the *b* sound in the passage from *On the Banks of Plum Creek*—"brighter," "blazed," "bounded," "bigger," "throbbing," and "burst"—gives the sunrise description a kinetic energy that is lacking in the sunset descriptions.

The cadence of Wilder's writing was not accidental. In a 1937 letter to her mother, Lane discussed at length the effect the sound of words had on the "weight" and rhythm of writing, what she called "a meaning in *feeling*."[20] Her mother responded with a despairing, "You see I know the music but I can't think of the words."[21]

Wilder introduces sound into her writing in many ways. Often she uses onomatopoeia. Her words are not especially innovative transcriptions of sounds; rather, they are common interpretations. But, the context of such sounds adds a dimension to them. In a description of Indian ponies, the sounds of the ponies' feet alliterate with the *p*'s of the preceding sentences and echo the rhythm of the ponies' gait: "Laura was excited about the ponies. There were black ponies, bay ponies, gray and brown and spotted ponies. Their little feet went trippety-trip-trip, trippety-trip, pat-patter, pat-patter, trippety pat-patter, all along the Indian trail" (*LHP,* 306).

Wilder does not attempt to translate the sounds the birds make but merely records what Laura hears, thus emphasizing the variety of sounds the quite alert Laura hears. She does, however, interpret the sounds as a language: the geese flying south carry on a conversation (*LHP,* 200–201), as do the birds on Plum Creek (*BPC,* 18).

Wilder also uses metaphor to relay sensory messages, particularly those that are unfamiliar to the readers. While Laura and Mary are playing hopscotch one afternoon, they hear the Indians in the distance, "chopping with their voices": "It was something like the sound of an ax chopping, and something like a dog barking, and it was something like a song, but not like any song that Laura had ever heard. It was a wild, fierce sound, but it didn't seem angry" (*LHP,* 265).

Wilder offers possibilities for understanding the sound, beginning with an implied metaphor, "chopping with their voices," which she then expands upon by stating the simile upon which the implied metaphor is based—"the sound of an ax chopping." Two more direct comparisons are given, "a dog barking" and "a song." The indirect personification of the sound as "angry" follows the description by comparison: by focusing first on the recognizable descriptions (every-day sounds in a twentieth-century child's life), Wilder enables children to have a basis for creating in their own minds the image of a "wild, fierce sound" that "does not seem angry."

Sensation that is unfamiliar to Laura is also relayed through simile. When Laura moves into the frame house at Plum Creek after months of living in the dugout, she cannot recognize a sound she hears one night. It seems to be "thousands of little animals scampering on the roof" (*BPC,* 124). It is the rain, which she could not hear in the dug-out, and which she has almost forgotten the sound of.

When Laura hears the blizzard winds howling around the house in town at De Smet, she identifies other sounds in them, sounds from her past. It is the only reference she makes in any of the *Little House* books to the preceding volumes:

They [the winds] sounded like the pack of wolves howling around the little house on the prairie long ago, when she was small and Pa had carried her in his arms. And there was the deeper howl of the great buffalo wolf that she and Carrie had met on the bank of Silver Lake.

She started trembling, when she heard the scream of the panther in the creek bed, in Indian territory. But she knew it was only the wind. Now she heard the Indian war whoops when the Indians were dancing their war dances all through the horrible nights by the Verdigris river.

The war whoops died away and she heard crowds of people muttering, then shrieking and fleeing screaming away from fierce yells chasing them. But she knew she heard only the voices of the blizzard winds. (*LW,* 187)

Laura is particularly scared because she recognizes the "voices" in the wind, and they are terrifying in their familiarity.

Laura is also sensitive to touch. She enjoys the feeling of mud squeezing up between her toes (*BPC,* 19) and pulling on her ankles (*SSL,* 78). When she strokes the furs Pa has trapped, she distin-guishes between them, noting that each animal pelt has its own char-acteristic texture (*LHP,* 233). Minnows nibbling on her feet make "a funny, squiggling feeling" (*LHP,* 111–12) or "a tickly feeling" (*BPC,* 20).

Wilder also uses crossovers from other senses to describe touch, taste, smell, and sound. In a visual description, touch is often implied: "The grasses were crisping yellow now" (*BPC,* 62). Taste has color and aroma: hoarhound candy has "a rich, brown, tangy taste" (*BPC,* 78) and ham frying has a "salty brown smell" (*FB,* 24). In winter, when Almanzo pumps water from the well, the water comes out with "a chilly sound" (*FB,* 63).

The emotions of Wilder's main characters, especially Laura, are often revealed in the personification of the environment. When Laura leaves the Big Woods, the little house is credited with the ability to see: "The shutters were over the windows, so the little house could not see them go" (*LHP,* 6). Wilder's little houses are capable of feeling: when Laura leaves the house in Indian Territory, "The little log house and the little stable sat lonely in the stillness" (*LHP,* 325). Laura's environment acts as a mirror of her own feelings, what Jean Piaget calls "introjection."[22] When she leaves the little houses, she feels a sense of loss and separation, and she sees these feelings reflected in them. And when she has not resolved her feelings about a new environment, the environment reserves its judgment about her. When she first views the surveyors' house, her exploration is tentative, and so is her response to the house. Because she has not accepted the house, it does not accept her: "It seemed to know that Laura was there, but it had not made up its mind about her. It would wait and see" (*SSL,* 143).

Nature is intensely personified in the *Little House* books. It is alive in the same sense that Laura is alive, and it can feel and act as she does. Thus, the wind is described as "crying because it could not get in by the fire" (*LHBW,* 44), the grasses on the prairie can "sing and whisper and laugh" (*LHP,* 112), and the earth can "breath[e] softly" (*SSL,* 67).

Wilder's descriptions of the prairie reflect Laura's attitudes. When Laura is secure, the prairie is a pleasant place to be. When she is afraid, it is menacing. The prairie seems to have an ability to change itself to echo her emotional state. When Laura is happy, the prairie is filled with music and dancing (*LHP,* 68), but when she worries, the prairie seems upset. When Pa and Mary and Laura are walking home across the prairie after a day at the abandoned Indian camp, the sun begins to set. Laura realizes that Pa does not have his gun, and the prairie takes on dangerous overtones, so terrifying that it seems to scare itself (*LHP,* 178).

When the entire Ingalls household seems to be in danger, such as during the uneasy time in Indian Territory when a confrontation between the Indians and the settlers appears possible, the menace of the prairie intensifies. No longer is it a warm, welcoming environment; instead, to Laura, it feels as if it is concealing something that is stalking her (*LHP*, 288). She transfers her fear of events occurring on the prairie to the prairie itself, and she mistrusts it, as if it were somehow responsible for the safe, orderly progression of her life being disturbed.

In much the same way, Almanzo's environment reflects his exciting day in town, when he has found a money-filled wallet, returned it, collected a two-hundred-dollar reward, opened a bank account, and been offered an apprenticeship with the wheelwright. So much has happened that time seems to stand still for Almanzo, and on the ride home, his surroundings echo this mood of suspension: "The air was still and cold and all the trees were like black lines drawn on the snow and the sky" (*FB*, 365).

The inclusion of sensory detail and the personification of environment are responsible in great degree for Wilder's skillful recreation of a time and a place that have passed.

Characterization

The characterization of the Ingalls family is carefully drawn. Wilder painstakingly edited her manuscripts to maintain character consistency, deleting material that drew credibility away from the characterization and strengthening sections that complemented established traits.[23] This may account for the disparity between the portions of the narrative repeated in *These Happy Golden Years* and *The First Four Years,* for the latter did not undergo the editing process that the former did.[24]

Although Laura is the main character in the series, Pa is the center of the family. His decisions, which he discusses with Ma in advance but which she rarely challenges, determine the future of the family. Despite his "wandering foot [that] gets to itching" (*THGY*, 138) and his unease with being settled, he keeps his family as his major concern.

Pa is in charge of the family's morale. His great store of songs keeps the family's spirits high when they are in the midst of a collective depression or when he senses that they are in danger of losing their optimism. By his music he engineers the family's disposition, including his own. "The Big Sunflower," for instance, is his "trouble song," which he sings in blizzards (*SSL,* 250; *LW,* 37, 124).

Pa has the ability to understand the prairie. He can interpret his surroundings, and often acts as a translator of the unknown or unfamiliar. One night during the long winter, he plays his violin, and the melody is a "strange" one:

> The fiddle moaned a deep, rushing undertone and wild notes flickered high above it, rising until they thinned away into nothingness, only to come wailing back, the same notes but not quite the same, as if they had been changed while out of hearing.
>
> Queer shivers tingled up Laura's backbone and prickled over her scalp, and still the wild, changing melody came from the fiddle till she couldn't bear it and cried, "What is it, Pa? Oh, what is that tune?"
>
> "Listen." Pa stopped playing and held his bow still, above the strings. "The tune is outdoors. I was only following it." (*LW,* 120)

Ma's attitude throughout the books is one of placidity. On the rare occasions when she does lose her temper or speak sharply, the family reacts with shock, as they do when she objects strongly to Pa's going with the other men in town to convince a homesteading farmer to sell them his seed wheat for food. They are all stunned, for this is a side of her they have never seen; she is "quiet but . . . terrible" (*LW,* 244). The experience apparently affects her, too, for her hand shakes as she pours Pa's tea afterwards, and the usually imperturbable Ma spills it, indicating her distress.

One of Ma's primary functions is acting as a foil to Pa's impetuousness. Her insistence upon a stable environment for the children reins in his desire to keep moving west in his search for the elusive freedom he so strongly desires. But her placid nature, her quiet acceptance of what life brings her, also helps quell his fervent reactions. She alone can soothe him when he becomes agitated, as she does when he loses his temper during the long winter and rails at a blizzard howling outside, waving his fist and shouting at it. With a few words, Ma calms him and restores his composure (*LW,* 288–89).

Both Ma's and Pa's speech is spattered with truisms. Ma's maxims express her philosophy of dealing with pioneer life: "There's no great loss without some small gain" (*LTP,* 102), "Never complain of what you have" (*LW,* 243), and "We must cut our coat to fit the cloth" (*LTP,* 107). All her mottos have a special pertinence to the particular needs of living on the frontier. At one point she expounds her philosophy, which perhaps explains how she has coped with prairie life and reconciled the losses it has brought her: " 'This earthly life is a battle,' said Ma. 'If it isn't one thing to contend with, it's another. It always has been so, and it always will be. The sooner you make up your mind to that, the better off you are, and the more thankful for your pleasures' " (*LTP*, 89–90).

Ma seems to be predominantly concerned with raising the children. Her conversation never focuses strictly on herself, and she guards others' conversation to insure that her children do not hear unsuitable language or stories that might frighten them. She also monitors her children's language and never hesitates to interrupt them to correct their grammar as she does when Carrie, stationed at the window, spies the county superintendent who is coming to give Laura her teaching examination. Carrie is nearly frustrated by Ma's interrupting the vital information Carrie is trying to relay, just to correct her grammar, and Carrie eventually skips the parts of the sentence that are grammatically difficult for her in order to get to the important part—that the superintendent is almost at their house (*LTP*, 303).

Ma also guards her children from vanity and believes that it can be avoided if one is not praised too highly. When Laura wears a new dress, Ma is cautious not to overextend her approval, and tells her that "pretty is as pretty does" (*THGY*, 163). Only on special occasions does Ma bend her rules. When Mary tries on one of her new college dresses, Ma uncharacteristically tells her that she is "beautiful" (*LTP*, 96). This rare show of approval is particularly revealing about Ma's character. It may seem as if she is favoring Mary, but Mary is blind and has no way to judge her appearance, whereas Laura can look at her reflection and judge for herself. The unusual compliment shows Ma's gentleness and tactfulness in reassuring Mary.

On Laura's wedding day, Ma compliments Laura, but does so with reserve, for Ma does not wholly approve of the black wedding dress ("You know they say, 'Married in black, you'll wish yourself back' " [*THGY*, 271]), and her somewhat superstitious nature tempers her compliment: "Even if your dress is black, you look perfect" (*THGY*, 279).

Ma places great store in the value of good manners. No matter where the family might be, on the prairie in a covered wagon or in a dugout on the Kansas plains, Ma watches the family's etiquette. When, in the midst of breakfast outside the wagon on the prairie,

Laura calls to a bird, Ma stops her, reminding Laura that even if they are alone, isolated on the grassy expanse of plain, proper manners are important and the rules of etiquette are to be followed (*LHP*, 40).

Pa's wildness complements Ma's passivity, and in like measure Laura's wildness complements Mary's passivity. The disagreements between the two sisters are a major motif in the *Little House* series. When they are little, Laura has difficulty overcoming her jealousy of Mary's golden curls, an envy that is in great part fostered by Ma's comments and actions. During Aunt Lotty's visit to them in Wisconsin, a fight breaks out between Laura and Mary, for Ma has told them to ask Aunt Lotty "which she likes best, brown curls or golden curls" (*LHBW*, 181). Aunt Lotty, who is put in an untenable position, answers gracefully, "I like both kinds best" (*LHBW*, 182). Later Mary brags to Laura that golden hair is prettier, and Laura slaps her (*LHBW*, 183).

The trouble between Laura and Mary goes deeper than just hair color, however, for theirs is a basic opposition of character. Mary is always obedient and never naughty, while Laura is the impulsive one whose acts often get her in trouble. Sometimes Laura's actions are brave and helpful, as they are when the cattle and oxen she and Mary are driving home trap the two girls on a rock. While fright immobilizes Mary, it spurs Laura into action, and she springs down from the rock in an almost automatic response to gain control of the situation (*BPC*, 47). Strong emotions tend to make Laura react, whereas they make Mary freeze.

Although Laura likes being outdoors, Mary is happiest inside the house and becomes snappish when she is forced to act outside her home. Her sense of humor also diminishes, and she fails to appreciate Laura's lighthearted poke at Mary's usually strict control of language:

"I declare, you eat more plums than you pick up," Mary said.

"I don't either any such a thing," Laura contradicted. "I pick up every plum I eat."

"You know very well what I mean," Mary said, crossly. "You just play around while I work."

But Laura filled her big pail as quickly as Mary filled hers. Mary was cross because she would rather sew or read than pick plums. But Laura hated to sit still; she liked picking plums. (*BPC*, 64)

After Mary loses her sight, the dichotomy of character traits strengthens. Mary has already been depicted as being smugly correct: "Mary was a very good little girl who always did as she was told" (*LHBW,* 181–82). When she is blind, she gains a certain gratification from being able to tell when Laura is misbehaving, and to tell Ma what she has "seen." When they are on the train to Silver Lake, Mary reports to Ma that Carrie is fidgeting and then exclaims that Laura is, too, and smiles "in satisfaction" (*SSL,* 17). But her satisfaction is not the result of getting her sisters in trouble, but in understanding that she is still capable and functioning in the family despite her blindness.

Before Mary leaves for college, she and Laura talk about Mary's predominant trait of "goodness." Their candid discussion provokes the startling confession from Mary that always doing what was proper when she was a child was her way of showing off, of "being vain and proud" (*LTP,* 12). Yet Laura realizes that Mary's goodness is innate; it comes from deep inside her. Laura also senses that somehow Mary's blindness has further contributed to her understanding of what "goodness" is, and that it comes from Mary's faith in God.

Mary's blindness, while it makes Laura realize how much she and Mary have shared, further separates them, for they no longer attend social activities together. Mary cannot attend school in De Smet. Thus Carrie and Laura begin to be close, and it is Carrie that Laura takes with her on her adventures.

Nevertheless, Carrie, like Grace, remains a minor character, perhaps because neither of the younger sisters has been with Laura through all the books; Carrie does not become old enough to be Laura's companion until *By the Shores of Silver Lake.* Too, Carrie seems weakened by the long winter, and Laura, who remains strong, becomes her protector, making their relationship not one of peers but of a guardian and her charge.

The characters of Pa, Ma, Mary, and Laura are carefully drawn to illustrate the alliances that develop within families. Laura and Pa share traits: both are outspoken, restless, and would rather be outdoors than indoors. Mary and Ma share traits: they speak with caution, would rather be settled than moving, and are happiest indoors. Laura and Pa take chances and relish risk, while Mary and Ma are careful and prefer not to gamble. The differences in the family members are revealed in their reasons for being happy about moving back to the claim after living in town: "Ma and Mary were glad because this was the end of traveling; they were going to settle on the homestead and never move again. Carrie was glad because she was eager to see the homestead, Laura was glad because they were leaving town, Pa was glad because he always liked moving, and Grace sang and shouted in gladness because all the others were glad" (*SSL,* 259–60).

The traits that each member of the Ingalls family exhibits are emphasized deliberately, for it is these traits that sustain each member through times that threaten their individuality or, more drastically, their survival. Pa's exuberance and Ma's reserve support them during the hardships of homesteading; their opposite natures temper each other's extremities. Mary's conformity and patience allow her to adapt uncomplainingly to the loss of her sight. She has always liked needlework, and she is able to take pride in the handwork she does after she is blind, for despite her handicap, she can continue doing what she enjoys. Laura's love for the prairie sustains her when, as Laura Wilder, she watches her and her husband's dreams shrivel with the wheat; it is this love that makes "her spirit ris[e] for the struggle" (*FFY,* 133). These traits identify the characters as individuals, while allowing them to interact, with their differences, as a family.

The Structure of the *Little House* Novel

As Wilder discovered, writing a multivolume novel presented a unique set of problems. One was sustaining unity throughout the series, which she achieved by concentrating on the characters. During the writing of *By the Shores of Silver Lake,* when the master plan for the entire work was complete, her correspondence with her daughter records the formidable task such an undertaking proved to be. Pa's storytelling in *Little House in the Big Woods* became a leitmotif for the series as Wilder purposely included at least one scene in each book in which he told a story,[25] although his later stories are not textually isolated as they are in *Little House in the Big Woods.*

Wilder's insistence upon accuracy compounded the problems. As she lamented to her daughter, she would have had a greater latitude in structuring the novel had she and Rose not begun with characters from Wilder's life.[26] Even the animals had to be considered. A note in the margin of an early manuscript of *By the Shores of Silver Lake* reminds her to "dispose of" Jack the dog, since children were still writing and wondering whatever became of Black Susan, the cat in *Little House in the Big Woods.*[27] Wilder also told her daughter, somewhat wryly, not to worry about accounting for every single character;

the only one the children had missed was Black Susan. Although she wanted to tie the last volume with the first, she overruled her daughter's suggestion that the cat in *Little Town on the Prairie* be somehow related to Black Susan.[28]

Another way in which Wilder achieved a stylistic unity was by keeping attention focused on the Ingalls family. All the members of the Ingalls family are dynamic characters. Although Laura is the central character, she is not the only one who grows and changes. The changes in Mary are the most obvious, for they are precipitated by the cataclysmic effects of her blindness.

One of the most unusual aspects of the *Little House* books is that not only do the children change, the adults also evolve over the span of the years. Their process is not so obvious, however, as that of the children, who are physically and developmentally changing quite rapidly.

The changes in Pa seem to be those that are thrust upon him, rather than arising from within. His restlessness is apparently never conquered, only contained. The experiences of the years of traveling and struggling do not show on him, although this may be due to what Anna Thompson Lee calls "a certain blindness in Wilder's vision" concerning Pa.[29] He seems to escape responsibility for the hardships the family undergoes in his constant search for "better things." Because he is seen through the adoring eyes of Laura, his character is drawn a bit idealistically. Yet it is consistent, and Pa's development is not so much in the way his character changes, but in the way he changes his behavior to fit the realistic needs of his family. From the beginning of the *Little House* saga, he has been future-oriented, and his dedication to his family dictates his final decision: they will stay in De Smet, not because he wants to, but because it is what his family needs.

The changes in Ma are more easily identified than those in Pa, because Laura has an objectivity in viewing her mother that she lacks with her father. In *Little House in the Big Woods,* Ma is a young woman, relatively untrammeled by the world; her eyes shine with anticipation when Pa tells her about the sugaring-off dance in the Big Woods. The years of trouble and setbacks take their toll, however, and through the series Ma laughs less and less.

Ma's identity becomes increasingly entwined with her family. She soothes Pa when he loses his temper, and chastises him when he forgets to guard his language around the children. Refusing to spoil her daughters, she rarely compliments them unless it is for a school achievement, and then it is done with reserve. Her early training as a schoolteacher seems to emerge in the later volumes as she becomes almost painstaking about the girls' language and behavior.

But as Laura enters her teens, the relationship between Laura and Ma begins to change. Although Ma seems more distant than ever, there are subtle indications that Laura is seeing her in a different light, although she is not fully aware of it. Two scenes are perhaps the most telling.

The first occurs in *By the Shores of Silver Lake,* when Ma and Laura wait for Pa to return from a potentially dangerous errand at the railroad camp one evening. As they sit in the darkness, they listen to the quiet night sounds around them: their breathing, the rustle of the wind as it ruffles the curtain and runs through the grass, the rhythmic little splashes of the lake on the shore. Their senses are heightened; Laura even hears herself listening.

Ma begins to stroke Laura's hair, a gesture betokening great familiarity. It is a prelude to a moment of what is for Ma an uncharacteristic intimacy. She tells Laura that the sun and wind are drying her hair, and she should brush it a hundred strokes each night. Although this seems like a criticism, and therefore quite characteristic of Ma, it is followed by a confidence, phrased almost symbolically, as Ma says that when she married Pa, she had "lovely long" hair (*SSL,* 87–88). It is her way of telling Laura that her life has changed her, and in the kind of symbolic language that those who are very close use, she warns Laura against the same life.

The other moment occurs during *Little Town on the Prairie,* when Laura and Ma make Mary's dresses for college. Laura, who has never liked to sew, has always assumed that Ma did. It is a revelation for her to notice the tension around Ma's mouth as she struggles with the woolen cloth and to realize that Ma hates to sew (*LTP,* 90). As Mary models the finished dress, Ma and her three oldest daughters discuss corsets. Ma tells Laura that she should wear her corsets to bed at night, and adds that when she married Pa, he could encircle her waist with his hands. Laura teases her that the fact that he no longer can apparently has not affected his feeling toward her, and although Ma reproves her for her brashness, she blushes and smiles (*LTP,* 94).

Such moments of free communication between Laura and her mother show their increasing awareness of each other as Laura becomes a woman like her mother. It is a slow and gradual process that occurs naturally within families; the relationship between parents and their children changes as the children become adults. These moments are, however, sprinkled into their lives; the change does not come about abruptly. Shortly after Laura's pert teasing of her mother and Ma's pleased reaction, the old relationship of mother-daughter is reinstated, as Laura shouts in dismay when she discovers that they will spend the winter in town, and Ma rebukes her for her unladylike speech.

The structure of the multivolume novel, while it did challenge Wilder's abilities, proved to be a wise choice, not only because it is unusual in the canon of children's literature but because it provided a framework that allowed Wilder to extend her cast of characters in the great pageant of the *Little House* novel.

"So Many Ways of Saying Them"

Wilder was quite aware of the subtleties of technique and of the importance of not relaxing her standards of craft. Rosa Ann Moore's textual studies show numerous instances of Wilder's struggling with a line or phrase, trying to get it to work precisely for her. Wilder addressed the issue in a speech early in her career: "You will hardly believe the difference the use of one word rather than another will make until you begin to hunt for a word with just the right shade of meaning, just the right color for the picture you are painting with words. Had you thought that words have color? The only stupid thing about words is the spelling of them."[30]

The writer has many choices in his or her work. Decisions must be made about vital aspects of technique, decisions that will determine the effectiveness of the work. The choices are numerous, and the measure of talent, one could suppose, lies in knowing which choice to make. Laura herself expresses the writer's dilemma when she discusses words and meaning with Mary:

"We should always be careful to say exactly what we mean," [said Mary].
"I was saying what I meant," Laura protested. But she could not explain. There were so many ways of seeing things and so many ways of saying them. (*SSL*, 58)

Chapter Eight
Conclusion

When the first of the *Little House* books was introduced in 1932, the United States was suffering from the Great Depression. The Midwest had experienced a lengthy drought, and city dwellers were generally no better off than the farmers. *Little House in the Big Woods* was a story of security—of a family united against outside forces. Each book built hope; despite the Ingalls family's setbacks, there was the metaphorical West, the horizon of hope. This hope sustained a nation of readers undergoing their own trials.

The books experienced a revival of interest in the 1970s during the run of the popular television show, "Little House on the Prairie," and its less popular successor, "Little House on the Prairie: A New Beginning" (NBC, 1974–83). The program, loosely based upon the main characters of the books, outraged Wilder aficionados with the liberties it took with the stories and the characters. For instance, a flurry of adoptions occurred on the television show. In an effort to appeal to boys as well as girls, Albert, a streetwise youngster, was added to the Ingalls family as Laura's adopted brother. When the characters began the inevitable process of growing up, more young children were adopted into the Ingalls family to replace Laura and Mary and retain the young audience. The Oleson family also adopted Nancy, in both appearance and temperament a copy of their daughter Nellie, who had married and moved out of town.

American history also received some alteration. If the *Little House* books created a second Laura Ingalls Wilder, once removed from the real one, the show created a third, twice removed from the reality of prairie life. This third Laura existed in a time warp, a stage of American history that had never existed.[1] In addition, contemporary problems, such as drug abuse and the struggle for recognition of the rights and abilities of handicapped people (which resulted in another addition to the cast, a husband for Mary; both were blind), often intruded into the program's script, creating historical incongruities and a jarring didacticism not present in the books.

Conscientious teachers and librarians, fearing that children would be disappointed by the disparity between the books and the television show, were prompted to warn children drawn to the books by the program about the differences, but, for the most part, children read and watched both with little apparent concern about any discrepancies. The very nature of television as a dramatic medium may be responsible for children's ability to distinguish the two versions. "Laura" of the television show was Melissa Gilbert, an actress playing a role: "Laura" of the books was Laura Ingalls Wilder, the "real Laura"—a differentiation that lent credence to the latter. The fact that television has always relied on actors in its entertainment programming made distortion an unavoidable aspect of the medium, and audiences made allowances for that. Too, the parents of many of these children had read the books when they were young, and undoubtedly clarified questionable points.[2]

To its credit, the television show did retain the books' emphasis on the family, which appealed to a nation of viewers exhausted by violence on and off the screen. It was a family program in the tradition of "The Waltons," a television show also based upon the childhood reminiscences of a writer (Earl Hamner, Jr., author of *The Homecoming* and *Spencer's Mountain*), and which ran from 1972 to 1981 on CBS. "Little House on the Prairie" and "The Waltons" both took place during periods in America's past, and both apparently rejected the concept that money was important to happiness, for neither the Ingalls family nor the Waltons were prosperous but considered their wealth to be the family. The programs stressed the values of the family and a fiery nationalism, which appealed to an audience already captivated by a romantic nostalgia for an era less hampered and complex than the present. The themes of self-sufficiency and family support in the broader arena of national identity were well suited to the time frame of the *Little House* saga; unfortunately, they were also well suited to mawkish sentimentality, and both "Little House on the Prairie" and "The Waltons" fell prey to an overdose of what had initially been their major appeal—sentimental nostalgia.

Whatever criticisms have been lodged against the television show, whatever the indignities it may have thrust upon the *Little House* books and their readers, it did spark a renewed interest in the books, such that sales of the books and interest in the life of Laura Ingalls Wilder continue beyond the demise of the television show.

The run of the television program coincided with a phase in American culture that seemed almost tailored for the success of a pioneer family's story, and this may also account for revival of the popularity of the books. The social revolution of the late 1960s with its ecological activism had evolved into a rustic "back to nature" movement, focusing attention on the pastoral virtues of country life. Politically the United States was rocked with scandal in government; and the unabashed pride in America displayed by the main characters of the *Little House* books (and the television program) seemed to reassure an audience that had had its national confidence shaken.

Too, for children the books address concerns that are parts of every child's life, no matter what era he or she lives in, no matter where that child lives. Many children found that they could identify with the sibling rivalry between Laura and Mary, or the desire of Almanzo to grow up a little faster, having experienced it themselves. Children appreciated that Wilder seemed to recognize that being a child is never easy; Laura's flaws, such as her jealousy of Mary's golden hair, indicated that Wilder understood how difficult and unfair life could be for a child, and also proved that Laura was not a character given to them by an adult as a role model for better behavior, but as a comforting and perhaps cathartic companion, a true peer.

Farmer Boy also addresses the complicated nature of childhood, and is one of the earliest children's novels to approach the subject of a boy's desire to be accepted as a man. In many ways it is like Joseph Krumgold's 1953 novel, . . . *and now Miguel,* which was awarded the Newbery Medal. Both Almanzo and Miguel admire their older brothers for their capabilities, which have gained them their parents' respect, and both Almanzo and Miguel try to hurry the process of growing up in an effort to be "big enough."

One of the reasons the *Little House* books have remained perennial favorites with children is that they are free of didacticism. Didacticism is all too frequent in children's books, as writers attempt to use literature as a means of instruction. When the story becomes subordinate to the message or informational content of the work, it ceases to be literature and becomes lesson. Wilder wrote the books, as she stated, to share with children the experience of living during an especially exciting time in American history so that they might know more about the background of their nation, yet this purpose is not allowed to overwhelm the story. The multidimensional nature of the *Little House* books prevents them from being thinly disguised history texts.

This absence of didacticism allows the reader to focus on the main character Laura and to see not only how the era affected her and her family but how each of them affected history, for history and people are fundamentally bound to each other. It shapes them as they shape it. Jean Fritz, author of biographies and historical fiction for children, observes, "We cannot afford to forget that the past is not just a series of events; it is *people* doing things."[3]

Laura is not a stock figure merely called in by Wilder to act out a part—"child of a settler"—in the pageant of the American frontier. She has a personality and springs to life from the page; her vitality stems largely from the fact that the author stresses her sensory reactions. While details such as those we glean from Laura's observations may, as Jean Fritz phrases it, "give the past its vigor,"[4] when such details are presented by a character rather than by the author, they also breathe life into the character.

As Laura watches her father make a latch for the door, the reader is receiving more than information about how door latches were made; the characters themselves are being revealed. Laura is identified as observant, interested in her environment and any events occurring within it or affecting it, and fascinated by her father's inventiveness and skill. Pa's characterization is enhanced as the reader learns that he is resourceful and adept with his hands. But scenes such as this do more than divulge additional traits of individual characters; they convey the necessary essence of the relationships the characters have with one another. The tone of this passage, for instance, reveals the emotional warmth and intimacy of the Ingalls home and the love that Laura and Pa have for each other.

According to Claudia Lewis, it is such warmth that characterizes those books identified as classics.[5] Warmth, the depth of feeling and caring about someone or something other than one's self, is necessary to make the reader care as much about the characters as the protagonist does. In works that are set in the past as the *Little House* books are, such human emotions are needed so that the reader can accept the characters as human beings not unlike him- or herself.

Early Wilder commentary is flawed somewhat because critics had difficulty identifying the genre to which the *Little House* books belong. During the popularity of the "Little House on the Prairie" television show, when much attention was directed toward Wilder, a wave of articles about her were published in response to the public's demand to know more about the pioneer heroine. Many of those who wrote these articles accepted the events and their arrangement in the books as the actual sequence of events in Wilder's life, and the resulting "biographies" of Wilder, based upon her own fictions, were little more than synopses of the books.

It was not always a matter of insufficient research; researchers were, in fact, encouraged to believe that the books were an actual recounting of Wilder's youth and discouraged from thinking otherwise. Wilder's daughter, Rose Wilder Lane, had earlier quickly and efficiently dispelled any doubt expressed or question raised about whether the events in her mother's life might be contrary to the published accounts.[6] A well-known writer and an accomplished free-lancer, Lane understood the impact of effective marketing on sales, and her fierce defense of the absolute veracity of her mother's books was perhaps a protection of what she saw as a merchandising advantage, one that separated the *Little House* books from the many other historical novels written for children, for the autobiographical aspect added commercial appeal as well as being excellent marketing material.[7]

Two definitions clarify the genre to which the *Little House* books belong. Alfred Tressider Sheppard explains that "an historical novel must of necessity be a story of the past in which imagination comes to the aid of fact."[8] Autobiographical literature is a form of historical fiction. Mutlu Konuk Blasing echoes Lane's distinction between "truth" and "fact" ("The truth is a meaning underlying them [the facts]; you tell the truth by *selecting* the facts which illustrate it")[9] by stating that autobiographical literature "does not imply any particular standard of 'truth' to the 'facts,' since the recording of a life necessarily represents the fictionalization—to a greater or lesser degree—of the life lived." Blasing also simplifies the working definition of the genre as "works in which the hero, narrator, and author can be identified by the same name."[10]

Because the *Little House* books are written for children, it is tempting to restrict any literary comparisons to the canon of children's literature. One critic refers to the work of Louisa May Alcott in discussing Wilder's writing;[11] and while it is true that *Little Women* is rooted in Alcott's life, the resemblance between that book and the *Little House* books is negligible. *Little Women* reflects an idealized vision of Alcott's life, what could have been, rather than what was.[12] The novel is so different from the events of her life that the characters are almost caricatures of their real-life counterparts. A contemporary of Alcott, Henry David Thoreau, provides a better basis for a comparative study of the artistic process of creating autobiographical fiction.

An outstanding example of the molding and shaping of experience to meet the demands of artistry is Thoreau's *Walden,* which underwent many of the same transformations from experience into literary form as Wilder's books. In autobiographical fiction, some changes are made so that the artistic intention of the author may be achieved. Thoreau found it ncessary to manipulate time to fulfill his intention in writing *Walden.* He compressed two years of living at Walden Pond into one fictive year to provide the literary unity he sought. The framework of a year provided a natural outline, and the cyclical aspect of the seasons added the structure he needed.

In the *Little House* books, Wilder combined her two stays in Wisconsin to create the one year of *Little House in the Big Woods.* If the "Pioneer Girl" manuscript is viewed as a strictly autobiographical account, therefore absolutely factual—or as factual as it is possible to be—in its recording of the events in Wilder's life and the sequence in which they occurred, many of the episodes appearing in *Little House in the Big Woods,* which precedes *Little House on the Prairie* in both publication and the chronology of the series, actually took place after *Little House on the Prairie.*

However strong the tradition of the autobiographical novel, some variations within the genre do exist. One of them is the type of point of view the author adopts. This is an especially important consideration in autobiographical fiction, for point of view contains clues to the reader about how the writer intends the work to be read. Thoreau chose to write *Walden* in the first person. Rebecca Lukens observes that "one of the strongest assets of first-person narration is its great potential for pulling the reader into what appears to be autobiographical truth."[13] The first-person mode served Thoreau well in his creation of a narrator who had discovered great spiritual truths in his metaphorical year at Walden Pond.

Wilder uses no narrator; to do so would be to place an emphasis on the truth of Laura's life rather than on the truth of Laura's situation. As Lukens also notes, Wilder's choice of writing in the third person establishes Laura as the "universal child," one who is recognizable in any time or any setting; such an identity can prove especially helpful when writing about experiences that are alien to the reader.[14] The use of the persona "Laura" places the experience of the *Little House* books in the timeless era that is the realm of fiction and invites children to engage in that curious phenomenon adults call "losing one's self in a book." The cliché is not without some basis in truth: if the protagonist is strongly drawn and believable, as Laura is, the reader's self will be surrendered to the personality of the main character. Through this transfer, the reader "becomes" Laura, and the experiences of the story become a part of the reader's experience. In reconstructing moments that belong to the province of the past, the atmosphere, the emotions, the total surroundings must be recreated within the reader's mind. Because the details are seen through the eyes of Laura or Almanzo, they gain a vitality for the reader who is, like the character, a child.[15] A character like Laura who exists in a world thus brought to life lives in the mind of the reader through the somewhat esoteric relationship offered by fiction, the transcending fellowship of being someone else for a while and vicariously learning and growing as the character does.

Only recently has Wilder's work come to be examined as regional literature. As Stephanie Kraft points out, Wilder shared essentially the same background as Willa Cather, Hamlin Garland, and Sinclair Lewis, yet each viewed and interpreted his or her background differently.[16] Garland and Wilder even lived in the same town, Burr Oak, Iowa, although at different times, and both homesteaded in South Dakota. Garland's work affronted other frontier settlers with its pessimistic view of prairie life, and one writer who knew the Garland family reminisced that Garland's memory seemed somewhat lapsed about his early life.[17]

Wilder's work differs greatly from Garland's in that hers presents a balanced vision of homesteading life; it is neither sentimentally joyous nor bitterly negativistic. The struggles with the forces of nature, particularly in *The Long Winter,* are countered by the sense of unison and affirmation found in the family. It is through this proportioning of experience that Wilder achieves what could be her greatest accomplishment: defining what power it was that kept people alive and sane when the elements seemed collectively conspiring to defeat them. Admittedly, Wilder's love for her family colors the way she sees adversity; in it she recognizes a test that strengthened already strong family bonding and helped her grow into a strong woman.

It would, however, be misleading to classify the Wilder books solely as midwestern regional literature: as Fred Erisman notes in his studies of the regionalism of the *Little House* books, they represent five settings.[18] Each place feels different, as Pa notes when they are traveling from Plum Creek in Minnesota to Silver Lake in the Dakota Territory (*SSL,* 60), and Wilder shows that in fact each is different. All the settings have particular features unique to themselves, and each area's singular characteristics have an impact upon the chain of events in the Ingalls family, as they traverse the plains in search of the final "little house."

The five settings of the books play integral roles in the themes of the books. The upstate New York setting of *Farmer Boy,* the most vaguely drawn of the *Little House* locales, shows a land that is fruitful, a land that, through years of farming, exists in symbiotic relationship with those who dwell on it. Yet the landscapes of the other *Little House* books reveal a more intimate relationship between land and people. In Wisconsin, the little log house is an island of security in the unknown surroundings of the Big Woods. In Indian Territory, the Indians are an intrinsic part of the landscape. Even when the Indians are not visibly present, the scattered beads Laura and Mary find and the sound of the Indians' voices filling the air add to Laura's feeling that this prairie is alive with the unseen; it has eyes and seems to be waiting. In Minnesota, the march of the omnivorous grasshoppers across the terrain destroys the settlers' livelihood and the Ingalls family's hopes for the future.

In the Dakota Territory, where the majority of the books are located, a series of images illustrate the magnitude of change wrought by people as they build the town of De Smet. Two images are especially vivid. The first is the peaceful scene of wild geese flying over the Big Slough and Silver Lake when the Ingalls family first arrives in the area. This image remains, providing a contrast to the same vista only a short time later after the settlers have left their mark. The second image is that of the people in the area crippled by a relentless onslaught of fierce blizzards, and this image illustrates that no matter what alterations the settlers have made to the landscape, there remains a part of it they cannot change.

Wilder creates a series of memorable landscapes, emphasizing the relationship of the land and the people, showing how one affects the other. The final landscape, that of the area around Silver Lake, adds the last note to Wilder's prairie panoramas by illustrating that both people and the elements, as parts of the landscape, have the capacity for destroying each other, as they very nearly do: the extremes of prairie weather prove to be the undoing of many settlers, who in turn drive away the native wildlife with the clamor of building the towns.

The emphasis upon regional identity does not mean that national identity is lost or undermined; rather, it draws attention to the fact that each area is an integral part of the American life and culture. As the Ingalls family anxiously awaits letters, magazines, newspapers, packages, and the materials of physical survival that must be brought in from other parts of the country, the recognition of the interdependency the settlers have with the rest of the nation is accentuated. The moving Fourth of July celebrations also stress the characters' strong awareness of a national identity. In *Little Town on the Prairie,* Wilder repeats the Declaration of Independence through the voice of the Independence Day speaker, and as Laura and Carrie listen, they mentally say the words with him. When Pa leads the crowd in the national anthem, Laura thinks about what it means to be an American, and the moment has an almost religious fervor about it.

The strong regional focus supplies Wilder's *Little House* narrative with important aspects that account for much of its success. The creation of what critics call "a sense of place," set in the larger environs of the United States, brings alive events that are part of its historical heritage, and shows what effects these had on a family—in particular, on a girl who was growing up in an era of change and whose discovery of a regional and a national identity helped her to define her own.

Notes and References

Chapter One

1. Laura Ingalls Wilder, Bookweek Speech, 1937, Laura Ingalls Wilder Series, Rose Wilder Lane papers, Herbert Hoover Presidential Library, West Branch, Iowa. Hereafter referred to as Lane Papers.
2. Rose Wilder Lane to Laura Ingalls Wilder, 21 January 1938, Lane Papers.
3. Wilder, Bookweek Speech, Lane Papers.
4. The biographical information in this chapter is collated from a variety of sources, including the biographical works listed in the Bibliography; interviews with the staff at the Laura Ingalls Wilder Memorial Societies; and material in the Lane Papers at the Herbert Hoover Presidential Library.
5. Laura Ingalls Wilder to *Public Opinion,* 18 June 1947, reprinted as "A Lovely Place," distributed by Laura Ingalls Wilder Park and Museum, Inc., Burr Oak, Iowa.
6. Wilder to Lane, [20 March 1937?], Lane Papers.
7. From outline of *Little Town on the Prairie.* Wilder wrote after these lines, "Fact! This was Manly's proposal and my answer." Lane Papers.
8. *On the Way Home* (New York: Harper, 1962), 24.
9. Ibid, 40.
10. Ibid, 69.
11. William T. Anderson, "The Literary Apprenticeship of Laura Ingalls Wilder," *South Dakota History* 13 (1983):307.
12. *West from Home,* ed. Roger Lea MacBride (New York: Harper, 1974), 4–5.
13. Lane to Wilder, late 1924, Lane Papers.
14. *West from Home,* 79.
15. Virginia Kirkus, "The Discovery of Laura Ingalls Wilder," *Horn Book* 29 (1953):428.

Chapter Two

1. Alan Dundes, *The Study of Folklore* (Englewood Cliffs, N.J.: Prentice-Hall, 1965), 2.
2. Francis Lee Utley, "A Definition of Folklore," in *Our Living Traditions,* ed. Tristam Potter Coffin (New York: Basic Books, 1968), 13. Unless otherwise indicated Utley and Dundes are the sources for the discussion of folklore in this chapter.
3. Wilder, Bookweek Speech, Lane Papers.

4. Bronislav Malinowski, *Magic, Science and Religion and Other Essays* (Glencoe, Ill.: Free Press, 1948), 82.

5. Fiery to Wilder, 12 February 1931, Lane Papers.

6. Lane to Wilder, 16 February 1931, Lane Papers.

7. After Mary loses her sight (between *On the Banks of Plum Creek* and *By the Shores of Silver Lake*), she shares storytelling duties with Pa.

8. Malinowski, *Magic, Science,* 82.

9. Elizabeth Nesbitt, "Hold To That Which Is Good," *Horn Book* 16 (1940):14.

10. Dundes, *Study of Folklore,* 3.

11. Pa also calls Laura "Flutterbudget," a name which he uses more frequently as she nears her teens.

12. Dundes, *Study of Folklore,* 3–4.

13. According to William S. Baring-Gould and Ceil Baring-Gould who identify the rhyme as a Mother Goose "charm," the tradition of assigning work by the day of the week is apparently based on the fact that the first washday on land after the *Mayflower* docked was a Monday. *The Annotated Mother Goose* (New York: Bramhall House, 1962), 219–20.

14. *The Real Mother Goose* (Chicago: Rand McNally, 1916), 87.

15. For a discussion of the American tradition of creating new lyrics for a preexisting melody, see W. Edson Richmond, " 'Just Sing It Yourself': The American Lyric Tradition," in *Our Living Traditions,* ed. Coffin, 94–107.

16. Hennig Cohen, "American Literature and American Folklore," in *Our Living Traditions,* ed. Coffin, 242–43.

Chapter Three

1. Wilder, Bookweek Speech, Lane Papers.

2. William Holtz, "Closing the Circle: The American Optimism of Laura Ingalls Wilder," *Great Plains Quarterly* 4 (Spring 1984):84–87.

3. William Appleman Williams, *The Contours of American History* (Cleveland: World Publishing Co., 1961), 257.

4. When the land was finally taken from the Indians, it could not be homesteaded; it had to be purchased from the government. See Robert V. Hine, *The American West: An Interpretive History* (Boston: Little, Brown & Co., 1973), 161.

5. In a letter to Rose Wilder Lane, 27 March 1933, Grant Foreman quoted an 1870 report by Captain John N. Craig of the United States Army at Fort Gibson to the Commissioner of Indian Affairs regarding the settlement of Indian lands by white settlers along the Verdigris River: "There is no doubt these people have been encouraged by the assurance of individuals on whose political influence and knowledge they rely, but had they been sure that the Government would protect Indian title to the country, it is al-

together improbable they would have intruded into it." Craig continues that the troops have arrived to remove "these intruders" and that "there is no reason for apprehending they will not accomplish their purpose." In Lane Papers.

6. The Homestead Act was designed to assist the government in set-tling—and thus gaining control of—the western part of the continent. The government was more successful in achieving its goal than were the home-steaders who hoped to earn their land: between 1862 and 1890, the popula-tion of the homesteaded areas grew by over 10 million people, while only 372,659 homestead claims were successfully completed. See Henry Nash Smith, *Virgin Land: The American West as Symbol and Myth* (Cambridge, Mass.: Harvard University Press, 1970), 190.

7. The fourteen dollars Pa paid was apparently an administrative fee, although ten dollars was the usual amount (Hine, *American West*, 161).

8. Between 1860 and 1900, the production of farm machinery esca-lated in the United States from a value of $21 million to $101 million (Hine, *American West*, 160). This drastic increase was undoubtedly due in part to the westward movement.

9. Holtz, "Closing the Circle," 84.

10. Ray Allen Billington, *The American Frontier* (Washington, D.C.: Service Center for Teachers of History, 1958), 21.

11. Frederick Jackson Turner, "The Significance of the Frontier in American History," in *The Frontier in American History* (1920; reprint ed., in *The Turner Thesis Concerning the Role of the Frontier in American History*, rev. ed. [Boston: D.C. Heath and Co., 1956]), 17–18.

12. Wilder, Bookweek Speech, Lane Papers.

13. Elizabeth Segel, "Laura Ingalls Wilder's America: An Unflinching Assessment," *Children's Literature in Education* 8 (1977):68.

14. Ray Billington, *Land of Savagery, Land of Promise* (New York: W. W. Norton & Co., 1981), 201–3. Billington also observes that this plundering of land encouraged mobility by forcing pioneers further westward in search of fresh "virgin fields."

15. Segel, "Wilder's America," 69–70.

16. Wilder, Bookweek Speech, Lane Papers.

17. Ibid.

18. Lane to Wilder, 21 January 1938, Lane Papers.

19. Billington, *American Frontier*, 22.

Chapter Four

1. Women also homesteaded. Almanzo's sister Eliza Jane, who also appears in the *Little House* books as Laura's schoolteacher, took a homestead near De Smet.

2. Julie Roy Jeffrey, *Frontier Women: The Trans-Mississippi West, 1840–1880* (New York: Hill & Wang, 1979), 25.

3. Ibid, 14–15.

4. Sandra L. Myres, *Westering Women and the Frontier Experience, 1800–1915* (Albuquerque: University of New Mexico Press, 1982), 151.

5. Jeffrey, *Frontier Women,* 38.

6. Susan H. Armitage, "Women's Literature and the American Frontier: A New Perspective on the Frontier Myth," in *Women, Women Writers, and the West,* ed. L. L. Lee and Merrill Lewis (Troy, N.Y.: Whitston Publishing Co., 1979), 9.

7. Edwin C. Torrey, *Early Days in Dakota* (Minneapolis: Farnham Printing & Stationery Co., 1925), 100.

8. See Wilder, "The Farmer's Wife Says," *McCall's,* June 1919, 8 and 62, for Wilder's view of the marriage relationship on a farm.

9. Beverly J. Stoeltje, "A Helpmate for Man Indeed," *Journal of American Folklore* 88 (1975):27.

10. Elizabeth Hampsten, *Read This Only To Yourself: The Private Writings of Midwestern Women, 1880–1910* (Bloomington: Indiana University Press, 1982), 38.

11. Glenda Riley, "Women in the West," *Journal of American Culture* 3 (1980):314.

12. Christiane Fischer, ed., *Let Them Speak for Themselves: Women in the American West* (Hamden, Conn.: Archon Books, 1977), 19–20.

Chapter Five

1. Wilder overruled her daughter's objections to the "adult stuff" Wilder had included in the drafts of *By the Shores of Silver Lake,* noting that Laura was growing up and had to be shown as such, reacting as an adult as well as a child; Wilder described her as "spotty." Wilder to Lane, 26 January 1938, Lane Papers.

2. For a full discussion of Wilder's dichotomous ordering and an application of the ideas of French theorist Gaston Bachelard (in *The Poetics of Space,* 1958) to the *Little House* books, see Dolores Rosenblum's essay, " 'Intimate Immensity': Mythic Space in the Works of Laura Ingalls Wilder," in *Where the West Begins,* ed. Arthur R. Huseboe and William Geyer (Sioux Falls, S. Dak.: Center for Western Studies Press, 1978), 72–79.

3. Jean Piaget, *The Child's Conception of the World* (1929; reprint ed., London: Routledge & Kegan Paul, 1951), 125–27.

4. Wilder to Lane, 26 January 1938, Lane Papers.

Chapter Seven

1. Lane to Wilder, late 1924, Lane Papers.

2. Kirkus to Wilder, 15 December 1931, Lane Papers.

3. Anderson, "Literary Apprenticeship," 298.

4. Ibid.

5. Rosa Ann Moore, "Laura Ingalls Wilder's Orange Notebooks and the Art of the Little House Books," *Children's Literature* 4 (1975):118–19, n.4.

6. Ibid.

7. Anderson, "Literary Apprenticeship," 299.

8. Ibid, 298.

9. Ibid.

10. Lane to Wilder, 16 February 1931, Lane Papers.

11. Lane to Wilder, 19 December 1937, Lane Papers.

12. Ibid.

13. Lane to Wilder, 21 January 1938, Lane Papers.

14. Wilder to Lane, 25 January 1938, Lane Papers.

15. Wilder to Lane, 28 January 1938, Lane Papers.

16. Wilder to Lane, 17 August 1938, Lane Papers.

17. Wilder to Lane, 19 February 1938, Lane Papers.

18. Wilder, Bookweek Speech, Lane Papers.

19. The British spelling here is the result of "these damn ignoramuses in publishing offices." Lane to Wilder, 1937, Lane Papers.

20. Ibid.

21. Wilder to Lane, 19 February 1938, Lane Papers.

22. Piaget, *Child's Conception,* 236, 242.

23. Rosa Ann Moore, "Laura Ingalls Wilder and Rose Wilder Lane: The Chemistry of Collaboration," *Children's Literature in Education* 11 (1980):101–9.

24. Anderson, "Literary Apprenticeship," 285–331.

25. Wilder to Lane, 25 January 1938, Lane Papers.

26. Wilder to Lane, 17 August 1938, Lane Papers.

27. Manuscript, "By the Shores of Silver Lake," undated, Lane Papers.

28. Wilder to Lane, 17 August 1938, Lane Papers. This letter indicates that the working title of the last planned volume was "Prairie Girl," which apparently became *Little Town on the Prairie* and *These Happy Golden Years.*

29. Anna Thompson Lee, " 'It Is Better Farther On': Laura Ingalls Wilder and the Pioneer Spirit," *The Lion and the Unicorn* 3 (1979):76.

30. Donald Zochert, *Laura: The Life of Laura Ingalls Wilder* (New York: Avon Books, 1976), 212.

Chapter Eight

1. Discussions of the show's deficiencies can be found in many television reviews as well as articles in the newsletter *Laura Ingalls Wilder Lore.*

See especially Jake Newman, " 'Little House' Divided," *Washington Post,* 12–18 October 1980; reprint ed., *Laura Ingalls Wilder Lore* 7, no. 1 (Spring-Summer 1981):5, and "Little House on the Prairie," *Laura Ingalls Wilder Lore* 4, no. 2 (Fall-Winter 1978):10.

2. The subject of children's ability to accept both versions has been the matter of some debate. Certainly much depends upon the individual child's environment and literary background. The stronger the parental guidance and the child's reading history, the easier it is for the child to accept discrepancies that may undoubtedly occur when literature is put in a visual format.

3. Jean Fritz, "The Very Truth," in *Celebrating Children's Books,* ed. Betsy Hearne and Marilyn Kaye (New York: Lothrop, Lee & Shepard, 1981), 86.

4. Ibid, 85.

5. Claudia Lewis, *Writing for Young Children,* rev. ed. (New York: Penguin Books, 1981), 113–14.

6. See Anderson, "Literary Apprenticeship," 287–89.

7. This is my own speculation, based upon material in the Lane Papers.

8. Alfred Tressider Sheppard, *The Art and Practice of Historical Fiction* (London: Humphrey Toulmin, 1930), 15.

9. Lane to Wilder, 21 January 1938, Lane Papers.

10. Mutlu Konuk Blasing, *The Art of Life: Studies in American Autobiographical Literature* (Austin: University of Texas Press, 1977), xi.

11. Fred Erisman, "The Regional Vision of Laura Ingalls Wilder," in *Studies in Medieval, Renaissance, American Literature: A Festschrift,* ed. Betsy Feagan Colquitt (Fort Worth: Texas Christian University Press, 1971), 165.

12. "*Little Women* is the story of the childhood Louisa would have had if her parents had described it," according to Martha Saxton, *Louisa May* (New York: Avon Books, 1977), 11.

13. Rebecca J. Lukens, *A Critical Handbook of Children's Literature,* 2d ed. (Glenview, Ill.: Scott, Foresman & Co., 1982), 120.

14. Ibid., 124.

15. Rebecca Lukens, "The Child, the Critic, and a Good Book," *Language Arts* 55 (1978):454.

16. Stephanie Kraft, *No Castles on Main Street* (Chicago: Rand McNally, 1979), 153.

17. Torrey, *Early Days in Dakota,* 80–84.

18. Erisman, "Regional Vision," 165–71. Erisman is also the author of "Regionalism in American Children's Literature," in *Society and Children's Literature,* ed. James H. Fraser (Boston: David R. Godine, 1978), 53–75, which also discusses Wilder's work as regional literature.

Selected Bibliography

PRIMARY SOURCES

1. The *Little House* Books

Little House in the Big Woods. New York: Harper, 1932. Reissued with new illustrations by Garth Williams, 1953. Reprint. New York: Harper, Trophy (paperback), 1971.

Farmer Boy. New York: Harper, 1933. Reissued with new illustrations by Garth Williams, 1953. Reprint. New York: Harper, Trophy (paperback), 1971.

Little House on the Prairie. New York: Harper, 1935. Reissued with new illustrations by Garth Williams, 1953. Reprint. New York: Harper, Trophy (paperback), 1971.

On the Banks of Plum Creek. New York: Harper, 1937. Reissued with new illustrations by Garth Williams, 1953. Reprint. New York: Harper, Trophy (paperback), 1971.

By the Shores of Silver Lake. New York: Harper, 1939. Reissued with new illustrations by Garth Williams, 1953. Reprint. New York: Harper, Trophy (paperback), 1971.

The Long Winter. New York: Harper, 1940. Reissued with new illustrations by Garth Williams, 1953. Reprint. New York: Harper, Trophy (paperback), 1971.

Little Town on the Prairie. New York: Harper, 1941. Reissued with new illustrations by Garth Williams, 1953. Reprint. New York: Harper, Trophy (paperback), 1971.

These Happy Golden Years. New York: Harper, 1943. Reissued with new illustrations by Garth Williams, 1953. Reprint. New York: Harper, Trophy (paperback), 1971.

The First Four Years. New York: Harper, 1971. Reprint. New York: Harper, Trophy (paperback), 1971.

2. Published Diaries and Correspondence

On the Way Home: The Diary of a Trip from South Dakota to Mansfield, Missouri, in 1894. With a setting by Rose Wilder Lane. New York: Harper, 1962. Reprint. New York: Harper, Trophy (paperback), 1976.

West from Home: Letters of Laura Ingalls Wilder, San Francisco 1915. Edited by

Roger Lea MacBride. New York: Harper, 1974. Reprint. New York: Harper, Trophy (paperback), 1976.

3. Selected Articles and Excerpts
"Favors the Small Farm Home." *Missouri Ruralist,* 18 February 1911, 3.
"The Farmer's Wife Says." *McCall's Magazine,* June 1919, 8, 62.
"Keeping House." *St. Nicholas,* August 1933, 473–75, 507–8.
"Indians in the House." *Child Life,* November 1935, 486–87, 511–12.
"The Land of Used-to-Be." *Christian Science Monitor,* 4 April 1940, 9.

4. Research Collections
Herbert Hoover Presidential Library, West Branch, Iowa. Rose Wilder Lane Papers. Manuscripts, extensive correspondence.
University of Missouri, Columbia. Manuscripts, some correspondence.
Laura Ingalls Wilder Memorial Society. All of the *Little House* sites and Wilder's home in Mansfield, Missouri, have been preserved or recreated. The most extensive collections are in Mansfield, Missouri, and De Smet, South Dakota. Two of the Memorial Societies produce newsletters: *Notes from Laura Ingalls Wilder Memorial Society, Inc.* in Pepin, Wisconsin; and *Laura Ingalls Wilder Lore* in De Smet, South Dakota.

SECONDARY SOURCES

1. Selected Biographical Works
Anderson, William. *Laura Wilder of Mansfield,* 1982. Available through the Laura Ingalls Wilder Memorial Society. Booklet covering the years 1894–1957, when Laura Ingalls Wilder lived in Missouri. Includes photographs.
————. *The Story of the Ingalls.* 7th ed. 1982. Available through the Laura Ingalls Wilder Memorial Society. Booklet detailing the lives of the Ingalls family and friends after the close of the *Little House* series. Includes photographs.
Lichty, Irene V. *The Ingalls Family from Plum Creek to Walnut Grove via Burr Oak, Iowa.* 1970. Available through the Laura Ingalls Wilder Memorial Society. Booklet covering the years 1876–78, during which the Ingalls family lived in Burr Oak, Iowa.
Warnock, Alene M. *Laura Ingalls Wilder: The Westville Florida Years.* 1979. Available through the Laura Ingalls Wilder Memorial Society. Booklet tracing and verifying the presence of Laura, Almanzo, and Rose Wilder in Florida, 1890–92.

Zochert, Donald. *Laura: The Life of Laura Ingalls Wilder.* New York: Avon Books, 1976. A simplified biography geared for younger readers. A bit too fanciful and vague with dates to be a solid scholarly tool, but it provides essential and useful biographical information. Includes photographs.

2. Selected Literary Studies

Anderson, William T. "The Literary Apprenticeship of Laura Ingalls Wilder." *South Dakota History* 13 (1983):285–331. Traces development of Wilder's writing and posits early dating of *The First Four Years.*

Barker, Roger G. "The Influence of Frontier Environments on Behavior." In *The American West: New Perspectives, New Dimensions,* edited by Jerome O. Steffen, 61–93. Norman: University of Oklahoma Press, 1979. Studies the relationship between the frontier environment and behavior of pioneers, drawing upon Wilder's work to provide supportive examples.

Bosmajian, Hamida. "Vastness and Contraction of Space in *Little House on the Prairie,*" *Children's Literature* 11 (1983):49–63. Approaches *Little House on the Prairie* from a phenomenological viewpoint.

Erisman, Fred. "The Regional Vision of Laura Ingalls Wilder." In *Studies in Medieval, Renaissance, American Literature: A Festschrift,* edited by Betsy Feagan Colquitt, 165–71. Fort Worth: Texas Christian University Press, 1971. Considers Wilder's work as a neglected example of literary regionalism.

————. "Regionalism in American Children's Literature." In *Society and Children's Literature,* edited by James H. Fraser, 53–75. Boston: David R. Godine, 1978. Discusses regionalism in twentieth-century American children's literature, with a heavy focus on the *Little House* books.

Holtz, William. "Closing the Circle: The American Optimism of Laura Ingalls Wilder." *Great Plains Quarterly* 4 (1984):79–90. Analyzes the tension between mythic and historic vision in the *Little House* books.

The Horn Book Magazine, December 1953 (special Laura Ingalls Wilder issue), 413–39. Reprint. A collection of several articles, including "Illustating the Little House Books" by Garth Williams; "Discovering Laura Ingalls Wilder" by Virginia Kirkus; and "A Letter from Laura Ingalls Wilder."

Jacobs, William Jay. "Frontier Faith Revisited: The Little House Books of Laura Ingalls Wilder." *The Horn Book Magazine* 66 (1965):465–73. Assesses the fundamental values and moral code of the frontier portrayed in the *Little House* books.

Lee, Anna Thompson. " 'It Is Better Farther On': Laura Ingalls Wilder and the Pioneer Spirit." *The Lion and the Unicorn* 3 (1979):74–88. Examines the characters of Ma and Pa in the *Little House* books from the standpoint of an adult reader and discovers a complexity of roles.

Moore, Rosa Ann. "Laura Ingalls Wilder and Rose Wilder Lane: The Chemistry of Collaboration." *Children's Literature in Education* 11 (1980):101–9. Identifies the influence of Rose Wilder Lane on the *Little House* books.

————. "Laura Ingalls Wilder's Orange Notebooks and the Art of the Little House Books." *Children's Literature* 4 (1975):105–19. Examines Wilder's writing process by comparing manuscript and printed versions of the *Little House* books.

————. "The Little House Books: Rose-Colored Classics." *Children's Literature* 7 (1978):7–16. Using Wilder's personal papers, traces Rose Wilder Lane's role in shaping the *Little House* books.

Rosenblum, Dolores. " 'Intimate Immensity': Mystic Space in the Works of Laura Ingalls Wilder." In *Where the West Begins,* edited by Arthur R. Huseboe and William Geyer, 72–79. Sioux Falls, S. Dak.: Center for Western Studies Press, 1978. Applies concepts of space and opposition developed by French theorist Gaston Bachelard in *The Poetics of Space* (1958) to the *Little House* books.

Segel, Elizabeth. "Laura Ingalls Wilder's America: An Unflinching Assessment." *Children's Literature in Education* 8 (1977):63–70. Examines the American experience presented in the *Little House* books.

Wolf, Virginia L. "The Symbolic Center: *Little House in the Big Woods.*" *Children's Literature in Education* 13 (1982):107–14. Studies the imagery and word choice in *Little House in the Big Woods* to discover a stylistic and structural "antithetical balance."

Index